MYSTERY MAN
OF
THE BIBLE

APOLLONIUS-THE NAZARENE

BY
HILTON HOTEMA

978-1-63923-443-1

Printed: October 2022

Cover Art By: Amit Paul

Published and Distributed By:
Lushena Books
607 Country Club Drive, Unit E
Bensenville, IL 60106
www.lushenabks.com

ISBN: 978-1-63923-443-1

MYSTERY MAN OF THE BIBLE

By

Prof. Hilton Hotema

* * * * * *

Chapter 1

HIDDEN LIFE OF JESUS

"Startling and shocking!"

"Those words are far too weak to express my feelings when I read the manuscript of the MYSTERY MAN OF THE BIBLE." -- Dr. F. S. C.

Orthodox Christians, smug in their conceit, little know that their Jesus is not what the literal statements in the Bible teach. They little realize that all of the New Testament is a parable, a fable, and that no one is competent to interpret that parable unless and until he has a good knowledge of the basic teachings of the Ancient Masters, as disclosed in our ten works, of which this is the last.

This series of ten folios covers the LOST WISDOM OF THE ANCIENT MASTERS, which is contained in the Bible in fabulous form, and is thus concealed from all except the esoteric.

Was the gospel Jesus man or myth? Did he live as a man, or did he represent on the Stage of Life the Cosmic Principles of the Universe?

Why does the Bible contain no dates as to his birth and death? Why was the date of his birth not known nor fixed until 532 A.D.? And why was December 25th selected as the date?

Why was it that the figure of a Lamb appeared on the Christian Cross until 680 A.D., when the Sixth Ecumenical Council, held at Constantinople in that year, ordained that, in place of a Lamb, the figure of a Man should be portrayed on the Cross.

By these facts of history, we learn when and at what period of time the story of the alleged crucifixion of Christ was formulated. We see that this story did not appear in the Bible until the year 680 A.D.

For sixteen hundred years the church, after it was founded in 325 A.D., has taught that Jesus was not only a man, a great man, the greatest who ever lived, but that he was the Savior of Mankind, "and washed us from our sins in his own blood" (Rev. 1:5).

It is strange that a man so great should have no history at all outside of the New Testament. It appears the only reason why the N. T. was written was to bring this Savior into being and give him some semblance of history.

There is strong suggestion of the Mystery Drama in the N. T. In the gospels the stage is set, Jesus appears, speaks his lines, and makes his exit.

But no actor, no mythical man, and no actual man has ever affected the world so profoundly as Jesus has.

Many great men have lived, and many pages of history are devoted to them, but none of these ever affected mankind so deeply as Jesus has, and yet he has no history except a brief story in the N. T.

Little is said of his birth and infancy. Then the gospels are silent and no mention is made of Jesus except in the Luke, when he was 12 years old. After that, the gospels are silent again until he is 30. Then for three short years he preaches to a few thousand people in a small region around Galilee, and disappears.

From all the evidence it is certain that Jesus was not a man. It is just as certain that someone called Jesus was invented for a definite purpose, and that such invention was the work of a great power with great wealth.

Only as such, with wealth and power back of him, could this character called Jesus have affected the world so widely and so profoundly. That fact we shall clearly show in this discussion of the MYSTERY MAN OF THE BIBLE.

The reader will be amazed to see how skilfully the Ancient Masters saved their Secret Science of Life from destruction and preserved it, in symbol and allegory, in the Fictitious Life of the Fabulous Christ Jesus.

Many despots and tyrants in the past had made vigorous efforts to crush the Sacred Science into oblivion. Constantine the Great was determined to have the job well done. He would invent a new religion, sell it to the people of his vast empire, and by this means weaken and destroy the Ancient Aracne Science.

But the Masters were too clever to be outwitted by this Roman Tyrant. They met him at his own game, and prepared the New Testament as he directed,--but they skilfully wove into the life of the gospel Jesus the Secret of the Stars, the Glory of the Sun, and the mysterious symbology of the Magic Wand of the God Hermes or Mercury.

For the blind exoteric, Jesus was the Lord and Savior of Mankind; but for the esoteric, he was the Symbol of Cosmic Principles and Spiritual Processes, one of which is revealed in his being crucified between two thieves.

There was nothing new about that. The sacred scriptures of the Masters always contained several meanings,--one intended for the masses, and the others intended for the initiates and disciples.

For sixteen hundred years the church has made billions of dollars by giving the world the exoteric message contained in the New Testament.

This work has been prepared to give the deceived reader the esoteric message of the Masters contained in the Hidden Life of Christ Jesus.

NEW TESTAMENT CODE CRACKED

After resisting all attacks of the critics for sixteen hundred years, the puzzling New Testament Code has at last been cracked.

The fact has at last been uncovered that the gospel Jesus was invented for a specific purpose, but not for that purpose preached by

-2-

(NOTE: this page has been re-typed from the original copy using our Selectric Typewriter. Thus the clearer print - and thus also the extra space).

the clergy.

The Masters made him appear to the exoteric as a man, while to the esoteric he appears in the true form as definite--

Spirito-psycho-bio-physiological processes of the body.

The Masters said, "As above, so below." They taught that the Macrocosm is composed of Great Soul and Great Body, and that the Microcosm is similarly constituted, being composed of Soul (Eternal) and Body (Temporal.)

It was necessary for the church to suppress and destroy this knowledge in order to make man believe in its doctrine of a Savior.

The Masters found that the spirito-psycho-bio-physiological processes in the body of the average man are practically dormant (dead) in their most vital centers, and could be "resurrected" by certain secret methods taught by them.

They never used the term "resurrection" to mean the return to life of a dead body. It was used to indicate the re-activation of what they termed the "dead spiritual centers of men."

It was the church that first used the term "resurrection" to mean the return to life of a dead body. Daily experience proves that to be false. No dead body ever returns to life.

The Masters said, In the "resurrection" (higher conscious state) men do not marry but are (without carnal desire) as the angels in heaven (Mat. 22:30), a subject we covered in The Red Dragon.

So the term "resurrection" means the re-activation of the dormant spirito-psychological centers of man, which causes his state of Consciousness to be raised, not from the dead, but from the dormant, narrow limit of the common five senses to the higher state of Seven (Seven Loaves), as are "the (consciousness) of the angels in heaven."

The top secret of the Masters was their discovery of how to "raise" man up from the Five Sense Plane to the rare Seven Sense Plan; thus giving him the powers of Clairaudience and Clairvoyance, when "there is nothing covered, that shall not be revealed; and nothing hid, that shall not be known" (Mat. 10:26).

Chapter 2

CHRIST JESUS

When was Jesus born?

Matthew: "In the days of Herod" (2:1).

Luke: "When Cyrenius was governor of Syris" (3:1-7).

Not one of the Evangelists gives the date of the birth of Jesus, but nearly every biographer gives the date of his subject's birth. Where do they get it?

Matthew and Luke attempt to give the time approximately. But between these two attempts there is a discrepancy of at least ten years; for Herod died 4 BC, while Cyrenius did not become governor of Syria until 7 AD.

Matthew clearly states that Jesus was born during the reign of Herod. Luke states that Augustus Caesar issued a decree that the world should be taxed; that "this taxing was first made when Cyrenius was governor of Syria," and that at the time of this taxing Jesus was born.

According to Matthew, Jesus was born at least five years before the beginning of the Christian era; according to Luke he was born at least six years after the beginning of the Christian era.

At least ten different opinions regarding the year of the birth of Jesus have been advanced by Christian scholars. Dodwell places it in 6 BC., Chrysostom 5 BC., Usher, whose opinion is most commonly received, 4 BC., Irenaeus 3 BC., Jerome 2 BC., Tertullian 1 BC. Some modern authorities place it in 1 AD., others in 2 AD., and still others in 3 AD.; while those who accept Luke as infallible authority must place it as late as 7 AD.

Matthew says that when the wise men visited Herod, he inquired of them as to the time when the star first appeared which announced the birth of Jesus.

When Herod determined to destroy Jesus and massacred the infants of Bethlehem and the surrounding country, he slew those "from two years old and under, according to the time which he had diligently inquired of the wise men," clearly indicating that Jesus was at this time approximately two years old.

In attempting to reconcile Matthew's visit of the wise men to Jesus at Bethlehem with the Luke narrative, which makes his stay there less than six weeks, it has been assumed that this visit occurred immediately after his birth, whereas, according to the Matthew, it did not occur until about two years after his birth.

Date of Birth

In what month and on what day of the month was Jesus born?

Not one of his many biographers is able to tell. Primitive Christianity did not know. The church was never able to determine this. A hundred different opinions regarding it have been expressed by Christian scholars.

What determined the selection of the date?

There was a double reason for it. In the first place, that date had been observed from a hoary antiquity as an ancient festival, following the longest night of the winter solstice, and was called "the Birthday of the Unconquerable Sun."

As we explained in the Ancient Sun God, at the time of the birth of the Sun, the sign Virgo; the Virgin, is rising on the eastern angle of the planisphere. Hence, all the Sun Gods are represented as being
-4-

born of a Virgin.

Another fact is that all the Mothers have names which mean or symbolize the sea, the Great Deep, thus: Mary, Maia, Maria, Meris, Myrrh, Mariam, Maritala, etc. The names all begin with M, which is also the symbol of the sign Virgo.

The fathers are all artisans of some kind,--carpenters, smiths, modellers, etc., indicating the active, creative power of the Sun, focussing the ruling aspect of the Creative Force of the Cosmos upon all Nature.

In all cases the birth takes place while the mother has been on a journey. So the Luke has Joseph and Mary travel "out of the city of Nazareth, into Judes, unto the city of David, which is called Bethlehem" (2:4).

Astronomically, the great star Spica (Arista) rises in the constellation Virgo, which rules Bethlehem (the House of Bread), with her companion Joseppe, in the constellation Bootes, and travels to a position in the heavens corresponding to the journey from Nazareth southward to Bethlehem.

Hence, the birth of the Sun Gods is announced by the appearance of a great star. And they are always visited by the Wise Men of their time who accord them divine honors and present gifts.

It was not until 532 AD that Dionysius Exigus, an Abbot and Astronomer of Rome, was commissioned by the Roman Catholic Church to fix the date of the birth of Jesus. then when December 25th was decided on, the Armenians and Syrians accused the Roman Church of Sun worship, because it adopted the date of the solar event--which was also the birth-date of the Sun God Mithras, of Tammuz, and all the other ancient Sun Gods.

So the doctrine of the Virgin Birth did not become a part of the gospels until the middle of the sixth century. The Disciples never mentioned it, and Paul, the greatest of the Apostles, never heard of it.

If Jesus had been born miraculously, all of Asia Minor would have known of it, and the ancient literature would be filled with accounts of it.

At the time of the winter solstice, after midnight on December 21, when the Sun has reached the lowest point of its descent into the souther hemisphere and begun its upward journey, the whole ancient world celebrated the birth of the New Year, and it is the same today.

On the first moment after midnight on December 24th, nearly all of the ancient nations celebrated the accouchement of the "Queen of Heaven" of the Celestial Virgin of the sphere, and the Sun God.

So it was an excellent scheme of the church to adopt and to celebrate on that day the birth of the physical Light-bringer in Nature, the Sun. And as one old belief after another was draped round the name of Jesus over the first five centuries of our era, so the Christian religion grew up in the likeness of the old. The ancient beliefs were hung on a new peg, called by different names, and the educated people were quite familiar with the sources when they came.

The second reason was, that at Rome the days from the 17th to the 23rd of December were devoted to unbridled merrymaking. These days were called the Saturnalia.

The church was always anxious to meet half-way the "heathens," whom it had converted or was beginning to convert, by permitting them to retain the feasts they were accustomed to, but giving them a Christian dress, or attaching a new and Christian signification to them.

Gibbon said: "The Roman Christians, ignorant of the real time of the birth of Jesus, fixed the solemn festival on the 25th of December, the winter solstice when the Pagans usually celebrated the birth of the Sun."

What precludes the acceptance of this date?

Luke: At the time of his birth, "there were in the same country sheperds abiding in the field, keeping watch over their flocks by night" (2:8).

Shepherds did not abide in the field with their flocks at night in mid-winter.

The Rev. Cunningham Geikie said: "One knows how wretched even Rome is in winter, and Palestine is much worse during hard weather."

Dr. Adam Clark wrote: "The nativity of Jesus in December should be given up."

The inability of the Christians to determine the date of the birth of Jesus is one of the strongest proofs of his non-existence as a historical character.

Were the story of his miraculous birth and marvelous life true, the date of his birth would have been preserved and would be today the best authenticated fact in history.

Where was Jesus born?

Matthew and Luke: In Bethlehem of Judea.

Aside from these accounts in Matthew and Luke as the nativity, which are clearly of later origin than the remaining documents composing the books and which many Christian scholars reject, there is not one word in the four gospels to confirm the claim that Jesus was born in Bethlehem.

Every statement in the four gospels, as well as in the Acts, concerning his nativity, is to the effect that Jesus was born in Nazareth of Galilee. He is never called Jesus of Bethlehem, but always Jesus of Nazareth. Also, histories and encyclopedias state that at the time of the nativity of Jesus there was no town nor city called Nazareth.

When Paul asked him who he was he answered: "I am Jesus of Nazareth" (Acts 22:8).   -6-

It was said that many of the Jews rejected Jesus because he was born in Galilee, and not in Bethlehem. "Others said, This is the Christ. But some said, Shall Christ come out of Galilee. Hath not the scriptures said, That Christ cometh out of the seed of David, and out of the town of Bethlehem, where David was"?--Jn. 7:41, 42).

That the man Jesus, if he existed, was not born at Bethlehem is affirmed by all critics. That he could not have been born at Nazareth is urged by many. Nazareth, it is asserted, did not exist at that time. Christian scholars admit that there is no proof of its existence at the beginning of the Christian era outside of the New Testament.

Philip said to Nathanael, "We have found him of whom Moses...and the prophets did write, Jesus of Nazareth, the son of Joseph" (Jn. 1:45).

"Search the scriptures; for in them ye think ye have eternal life: and they are they which testify of me" (Jn. 5:39).

The miraculous conception was in fulfillment of what prophecy?

Matthew: "Now all this was done, that it might be fulfilled which was spoken of the Lord by the prophet, saying, Behold, a virgin shall be with child, and shall bring forth a son, and they shall call his name Emmanuel" (1:22, 23).

This is esteemed the "Gem of the Prophecies," and appears in the seventh chapter of Isaiah.

The facts are these: Rezin, king of Syria, and Pekah, king of Israel, had declared war against Ahaz, king of Judah. God assured Ahaz that they should not succeed, but that their own kingdoms should be destroyed by the Assyrians.

To convince him of the truth of this, he requested Ahaz to demand a sign. "But Ahaz said, I will not ask, neither will I tempt the Lord...Therefore, the Lord himself shall give you a sign; Behold, a virgin shall conceive, and bear a son, and shall call his name Emmanuel....Before the child shall know to refuse the evil, and choose the good, the land that thou abhorrest shall be forsaken of both her kings."

In the succeeding chapter the fulfillment of this prophecy is recorded: "And I went unto the prophetess; and she conceived, and bare a son. Then said the Lord to me, Call his name Mahershalal-hash-baz. For before the child shall have knowledge to cry, My father, and my mother, the riches of Damascus (capital of Rezin's kingdom) and the spoils of Samaria (capital of Pekah's kingdom) shall be taken away before the king of Assyria."

Rezin and Pekah were overthrown by the Assyrians before 720 BC. Thus the two kings whom Ahaz abhorred were out of the way.

By using the symbolical term "Emmanuel" Isaiah assured them that "God is with us," for that is the meaning of the name given to the child. But Mary's child was called Jesus as the Lord instructed Joseph in his dream, and was never called Emmanuel.

Isaiah's prophecy of the virgin birth was fulfilled during the reign of Ahaz, and had no reference to Jesus and his mother. The conclusion is that Matthew falsely applied the prophecy to the birth of Jesus.

Virgin Birth

One of the most convincing proofs of Christ's divinity, with many people, is the supposed fact that he was born of a virgin and that his miraculous birth was foretold by a prophet seven hundred years before the event occurred.

There is not a passage in the Jewish Scriptures declaring that a child should be born of a virgin. The word translated "virgin" does not mean a virgin in the accepted, literal sense of the term, and that fact is stated in the Catholic Encyclopedia. It means a young woman, whether married or not.

The whole passage is a mistranslation. The words rendered "a virgin shall conceive and bear a son" should read, "A young woman is with child and beareth a son."

In this so-called prophecy there is not the remotest reference to a miraculous conception and a virgin-born child.

Next to the preceding, the following is most frequently cited as a Messianic prophecy: "The scepter shall not depart from Judah... until Shiloh come" (Gen. xlix, 10).

If Shiloh refers to Jesus, the prophecy was not fulfilled. For the scepter did depart from Judah 600 years before Jesus came.

But Shiloh did not refer to a Messiah, nor to any man. It was the seat of the national sanctuary before it was removed to Jerusalem.

This so-called prophecy, like the preceding one, is another mistranslation. The correct reading is as follows: "The preeminence shall not depart from Judah so long as the people resort to Shiloh."

"For unto us a child is born, unto us a son is given; and the government shall be upon his shoulder; and his name shall be declared Wonderful, Counsellor, The Mighty God, the everlasting Father, the Prince of Peace" (Isa. 9:6).

Prof. Cheyne, the highest authority on Isaiah, pronounces this a forgery.

It is a self-evident forgery. No Jewish writer could have written it. To have declared even the Messiah to be "The mighty God, the everlasting Father" would have been the rankest blasphemy, a crime the punishment of which was death.

The alleged Messianic prophecies in the Bible are Christian and not Jewish. Christian translators and exegetists have altered and distorted the biblical passages and perverted their meaning to try to make them refer to Jesus.

Christian theologians pretend to recognize in the Old Testament

-

two kinds of Messianic prophecies: (1) Specific predictions concerning Jesus which were literally fulfilled; and (2) Passages in which the author refers to other persons or events, but which God, without the author's knowledge, designed as types of Christ.

The fallaciousness of the former have been exposed--it having been shown that there is not a text in the whole Jewish Scriptures predicting the coming of Christ--they now rely chiefly upon the latter to support their claims.

These "prophecies" are almost limitless; for a firm believer in prophecy can, with a vivid imagination, take almost any passage and point out a fancied resemblance between the thing it refers to and the thing he wants confirmed; apparently oblivious to the fact that the passage is equally applicable to a thousand other things.

Had the Mormons accepted Joe Smith as a Messiah instead of a prophet, they would have no lack of prophecies to support their claims; and by translating and revising the scriptures to suit their views, as the church fathers did, these prophecies would fit him as well as they do the Christ.

House or Stable

Was Jesus born in a house or in a stable?

Matthew: "And when they were come into the house, they saw the young child with Mary his mother" (2:2).

Luke: "And she brought forth her first born son, and wrapped him in swaddling clothes, and laid him in a manger" (2:7).

Luke's account concerning the place of Mary's accouchement has been received, while that of Matthew has been ignored.

Christ's birth in a barn and his death on the cross are the lodestones that have attracted the sympathies of the world, and kept him on the throne of Christendom; for sentiment rather than reason dominates mankind.

Referring to the Luke story, the "Bible for Learners" says:

"Such is the well-known story of the birth of Jesus, one of the most deeply significant of all the biblical legends. That it is only a legend, without the smallest historical foundation, we must, of course, admit" (Vol. 3:pp. 54).

Justin Martyr states that Jesus was born in a cave, and this statement Farrar is disposed to accept: "Justin Martyr, the Apologist, who, from his birth at Shechem, was familiar with Palestine, and who lived less than a century after the time of our Lord, places the scene of the nativity in a cave.

"This is, indeed, the ancient and constant tradition, both of the eastern and western churches, and it is one of the few to which, though unrecorded in the gospel history, we may attach a reasonable probability" (Life of Christ, p.3).

In the Ancient Sun God we wrote: "All solar gods and saviors are represented as being born in a cave or a dungeon. This scene symbolizes the darkness from which the Sun rises in the morning.

"As the Dawn springs fully armed from the forehead of the cloven sky, so the eye first discerns the blue horizon of heaven as the first faint arch of light gleams in the east. This arch is symbolized by the Cave in which the infant is born."

Jesus was taken by Nazareth. Why? Matthew: "That it might be fulfilled which was spoken by the prophet. He shall be called a Nazarene" (2:23).

The Bible contains no such prophecy Fleetwood admits that "the words are not to be found" in "the prophetical writings," and Farrar says, "It is well known that no such passage occurs in any extant prophecy" (Life of Christ, p.33).

The only passage to which the above can refer is Judges xiii,5. Here the child referred to was not to be called a Nazarene, but a Nazarite.

The author of the Matthew knew that "Nazarene" and "Nazarite" were no more synonymous than "Jew" and "priest."

A Nazarene was a native of Nazareth. A Nazarite was one consecrated to the service of the Lord. The author of the Matthew likewise knew that this Nazarite referred to in Judges was Sampson.

John the Baptist is said to have been the person sent to announce the mission of Christ. Who was John the Baptist?

Jesus: "This is Elias, which was for to come" (Mat. 11:14).

John: "And they asked him (John the Baptist), what then? Art thou Elias? And he saith, I am not" (Jn. 1:21).

Here is a question of veracity between Jesus and John.

The Twelve Apostles

Twelve Apostles are named in the three synoptic gospels, but not in the John. This important omission is admitted to be a grave defect in the fourth gospel.

From the synoptic gospels the conclusion is inevitable that if there was one disciple whom Jesus esteemed higher than the others, it was Peter.

John, on the other hand, assuming that he wrote the fourth gospel as claimed, takes frequent occasion to impress us with the idea that he was the particular bright star in the Apostolic galaxy. Four times (13:23; 19:26; 20:2; 21:20) he declares himself to be "the disciple whom Jesus loved."

If John wrote the fourth gospel, this self-glorification proves him to have been a despicable egotist; if he did not write it, then the fourth gospel is a forgery. The first assumption, if correct, impairs its credibility; the latter destroys its authenticity.

Chapter 3

LIFE OF APOLLONIUS

If Jesus was a myth, who played the humanistic role assigned to him in the gospels?

That great philosopher, mystic, and magacian, Apollonius of Tyana.

The church destroyed so thoroughly and so well all writings by Apollonius and all writings regarding him, that what was written about him by his beloved disciple, Damis, we can never know; for even such portions of it which Philostratus used in his biography of Apollonius have not been permitted to come down to us.

While there is clear evidence of suppression more or less considerable in extent all through the work by Philostratus, there is a gap of twenty years in the Life of Apollonius by Philostratus which covers the part of it during which he was more active and gained most of his great renown as a prophet, preacher, medium and worker of miracles.

Most significant of all, this gap it is that covers nearly the whole of what was called the period of the teachings of Jesus, which the Apostles later continued.

Had the Memories of the Life of Apollonius be Damis, and the biography of Apollonius by Philostratus, been permitted to come down to us as they were written, there would not today be a vestige of Christian superstition in existence.

The one work has been entirely destroyed, and the other mutilated in the most diabolical manner, in order to hold the human mind in the thrall of a delusion that has prevented mankind from rising above the plane of heartless selfishness, despairing ignorance, grovelling debasement and inhuman tyranny.

The Neo-Platonist

Plotinus was a member of the school known as the Neo-Platonic, but which was also called the Eclectic.

The founder of this school was Ammonius The Peripathetic;but the person who really furnished the materials for the school was Apollonius; and all the ideas which that school gave forth under Potamon, Ammonius Saccas and Plotinus were gathered from the originals of the school of the famous Hindu, Deva Bodhisatoua.

His writings were the foundation, combined with some Platonic writings, which formed the whole of what the Eclectic school taught.

In the first place, the whole history of Jesus, so-called, was started by that Hindu representing the life of Buddha, and afterwards taught by Apollonius, who was the real Jesus of the New Testament. But that Hindu works were destroyed by the church.

-11-

In other words, the original source of all that is called Christianity was the Scriptures of Buddhism, introduced into Asia Minor and Europe by Apollonius, and later modified by Amonius the Peripathetic, Potamon, Amonius Saccas, and Plotinus himself.

Pope Gregory VII, in the 11th century, had destroyed the Library of the Palatin Apollo, which contained all the writings of the School of Alexandria from the early part of the first to the middle of the fourth century, the excuse offered being that he did not want the clergy to have their minds diverted from their "holy" work by studying heathen literature.

But the real reason was that there were recorded in that library all the facts which would prove that no such person as Jesus of Nazareth ever existed.

Who Was Jesus

J. M. Roberts, a lawyer who was born in Montgomery Co, Penna., in 1821, was one man who appears to have dug deeper than any one else in his efforts to discover the facts about Christianity and its Jesus.

In 1878 he founded his weekly journal titled Mind and Matter, and in it he published from time to time his findings on the subject. After his death in 1888, these findings were published in 1894 by the Oriental Publishing Company, and the book of 608 pages of rather small type was titled "Antiquity Unveiled."

This work shows that Apollonius of Tyana was the Jesus of the gospels, the Paul of the Epistles, and the John of Revelation. But the work failed to show that Jesus was also an actor, and played many parts on the Stage of Life, as shown by Kenyon Klamonti in his great work of five volumes titled "Awaken the World Within."

Apollonius was born February 16, the year 2 A.D., of wealthy parents, He was educated, until his 26th year, in general philosophy and literature, and served six years under Euxenes of Heracleia, learning the Pythagorian philosophy.

After acquiring all he could learn from the teachings of that philosopher, he went to Antioch, and from there to Jerusalem.

On account of some wonderful physical manifestations of spiritual power taking place thru his then young mediumship, which persons living in Jerusalem had heard of, his entrance to that city was hailed, as it was alleged the entrance of Jesus was hailed, with hosannas and songs of praise to one who came in the name of the Lord. This took place when he was 33 years old.

Nine epistles were given to him by Phraotes of Taxila, between Babylon and India, who was a satrap in those days. These epistles contained all that is embraced in the present epistles claimed to have been written by the biblical Paul.

Apollonius retired to the isle of Patmos, remaining there during the years 69 and 70, and while there he copied and edited a Hindu scroll that became the Book of Revelation in the New Testament.

-12-

Damis

Damis, mentioned in the Bible, was the beloved disciple of Apollonius, and wrote a biography of his Master which was destroyed by the church fathers.

Damis was an Ephesian, born in the city which was the chief seat of the worship of the Great Diana of the Ephesians.

Apollonius and Damis were both mediums, and in their presence materialized spirits appeared. When both were together, the spirit manifestations that occurred were stronger.

Damis reports that Apollonius made two journeys to India, the first about 36 AD and the last about 45 AD. On these journeys to India he obtained extracts from the Hindu gospels.

The first attempt of Apollonius to introduce the religion of Krishna in Western Asia was made shortly after his return from India, at Nazarita, a small village near Gaza. He there formed a community according to the Gymnosophic ideas and practices. The principle of initiation is expressed in that famous text in the Bible where it is said, "Thou art a priest after the order of Melchisedec." The original meaning of that was, "A priest after the order of the Sun."

It was also the Parsee worship and was derived from the "Golden Rule" of Hermes Trismegistus, whose writings contained the expression, "Thou art a priest Mechel forever after the order of the Sun."

Damis wrote memoirs of Apollonius from 34 to 80 AD, and these were mutilated by the Greek followers of Prometheus. Damis was called Timotheus by the Thesalonians.

Apollonius was the founder of the Nazarite sect said Damis. The word Nazarite meant to clear off the head bare.

In referring to the Essenes required the candidate to pass thru two flames, one a bright one and the other a pale one.

The reason that Josephus made no mention of Apollonius was due to the fact that they were initiated in the secret order called the "Sons of the no external relation to one another, so that if the brethren of the order had occasion to favor one another, or afford mutual protection in times of trouble and danger, their secret relations should not be known.

Very little can be gleaned from biographical or historical sources concerning Damis, and very little of that can be relied upon, on account of the efforts that have been made by the church to conceal everything possible that was true in relation to Apollonius and his Nazarite disciples.

Damis was a Greek historian, of Assyrian origin. He wrote in the first century AD, and was an inhabitant of New Nineveh. He joined Apollonius in that city, and accompanied him in his journeys. He wrote an account of these in which he inserted the discourses and prophecies of his Master. This work seems to have served as the basis of the Life of Apollonius by Philostratus.

Damis was a companion of Apollonius during his first imprisonment at Rome (AD 41), called by him his fellow laborer, Syneagos, in Philemon, 24; see also Col. 4:14.

It is impossible now to judge how far the writings of Apollonius came into the hands of Marcion and Lucian in their original shape. Those two men being none other than Mark and Luke of the synoptical gospels. It is equally impossible to know to what extent the latter altered them before they fell into the hands of Eusebius of Caesarea, the first Christian historian, and his contemporaries and coadjutors of the Nicean Council.

It is enough to know that in spite of all this changing and modifying by the priests of Prometheus, and the fathers of the church, the Apollonian or Essenian Christosism of India is shown to pervade it from beginning to end, and that there is nothing original or true connected with it as a distinctive or original religion.

It seems certain that through the testimony of Damis, we have been taken to the source of Christianity, which we find to have been India, and that instead of its having any relation to Jesus of Nazareth, it relates to the Hindu savior Krishna; and was taken to the Roman empire by Apollonius about the same time when it is alleged the mission of Jesus Christ began.

Father of Christianity

Who was the Father of Christianity? Marcion (Mark). He began the movement which led up to the founding of the Roman State Church.

He discovered at Antioch the so-called Pauline Epistles and took them to Rome, where he revised, changed, distorted and interpolated them to suit himself, for his own benefit and personal aggrandizement, he said.

Being a scholar, and realizing that these epistles contained facts not known to the world at large, he saw that they presented a rare opportunity to offer them as his own and make him great.

So he copied and edited the epistles from the originals by Apollonius; and in order to disguise the identity of their real author, he interpolated that description of Paul which was later copied by Lucian (Luke).

The principal foundation of the epistles was the zodiac sign Aries, the Ram or Lamb; and the early Christians worshipped a Lamb on a cross instead of a man, as previously stated.

So Marcion (Mark) was the first one to introduce these epistles to public notice, which he did about 130 A.D.

Thus the epistles attributed to Paul by the church were actually the epistles of Pol, Polos, Apollo, Apollonius, and were found by Marcion at Antioch some thirty years after the death of Apollonius about 102 A.D. Marcion took them to Rome, and by their use he hoped to become the head of a new religion by establishing a new canonical scripture. The new religion was formed, but not until after his death.

The writings of Apollonius were in the Samaritan tongue, and were not available to the Greek and Latin scholars of that time. It required an educated Cappodocian, as Marcion was, to translate them into the Greek and Latin tongues, with both of which he was as familiar as with his own.

The gospel of Marcion (Mark) is the original from which the church fathers fabricated the Matthew and the Luke.

There was a Gospel of Paul (Pol), and Apollonius was the author of it.

This gospel was Apollonius' version of the Sanscrit Gospel of Dave Bodhisatoua, obtained by him at Singapore, and modified by him in accordance with his own philosophic views.

It was this Buddhistic gospel of Apollonius that was still further modified by Marcion in the gospel which he preached in Rome. And it was still further modified some years later, and labelled the Gospel according to Luke.

In speaking of the loss or destruction of the evidence, Charles B. Waite wrote:

"Christianity has suffered no greater loss, than that of the writings of Marcion, the great theological thinker of the second century--the compiler of the first complete gospel--the collector of the epistles of Paul--the editor and publisher of the first New Testament.

"While the elaborate work against him, written by Tertullian, who called him a 'hound', has been preserved, and the work of Epiphanius, who bestowed upon him the euphonius appellation of 'beast', the writings of Marcion have perished, except such as are found in the references and citations of his adversaries. His works have shared the common fate of those of the heretics of the second century, none of which, in their original form, have been permitted to come down to us.

"Marcion was an educated man, and a profound thinker, and no relic of Christian antiquity, next to the epistles of Paul, would be more valuable than his writings. Being himself a collector of gospel and New Testament manuscripts, his writings upon those subjects would forever set at rest the question as to what gospels were then in circulation."--Ant. Unveiled, pp. 156.

Lucian (Luke)

Lucian (Luke) an educated Greek Satirist, received his description of Paul from Marcion; but was known to Lucian as Apollos in the Greek and as Paulus in the Roman tongue.

It was understood by all scholars at the time he wrote, that his writings referred to the life, travels and miracles of Apollonius, the oracle of Vespasian.

He merely followed the statements of Marcion, although he knew his statements were not correct, and never suspected that his description of Apollonius would be seized upon by Christians in after ages to perpetuate their fraud.

He was of a satirical disposition of mind, and it made no difference to him whether what he wrote was true or false. It was with him as with subsequent dramatic writers; and it mattered not what events he sought to use, whether sacred or historical, so he could make them suit his purposes.

Lucius of Cyrene

Lucius was one of the disciples of Apollonius, and had three different names, owing to the different languages in which it was written--Lucius, Lucas and Luke.

He was the writer or transcriber of the Life of Apollonius, as indicated by Damis, who was the beloved disciple of Apollonius, He helped Damis to write all those epistles in the New Covenant.

Lucius is referred to at first as Lucius of Cyrene in Acts 13:1. The second place he is referred to is in Rom. 16:21. He is also referred to in Col. 4:14 as "Luke the beloved physician," and in Phil. verse 24, as Lucas.

There is not a version of what is called the New Testament that is older than the latter half of the fourth, or the beginning of the fifth century. If there were older versions of the N. T., what have become of them?

It is evident that the oldest versions now extant were derived from the older versions, but no one knows how closely they followed the older versions from which they were copied.

A Dangerous Book

We have mentioned the Life of Apollonius by Philostratus, which he wrote in the early part of the third century.

After the gospel Jesus was invented in 325 AD., the first act of the church fathers was to burn all writings they could find, especially those of the first three centuries, which mentioned Apollonius as the great spiritual leader of the first century.

That is the reason why the ancient libraries were burned including the famous Alexandrian Library, which was burnt under the edict of the Emperor Theodosius.

The chief Librarian, being warned of the plot, secretly removed from the library some of the most valued writings and sent them to the east for safety. Among these was the Life of Apollonius by Philostratus.

From the burning of the Alexandrian Library until the suppression of Blount's first English translation of the Life of Apollonius, the church had made every effort to destroy this work, but failed.

During the Dark Ages this work was preserved by the Arabs, and was not introduced into Europe until early in the 16th century, when it was immediately put under ecclesiastical ban, with the result that at this time, even among the well educated, there prevails in the western world a general ignorance of the very existence of the Great Master of the first century.

The "Life of Apollonius" was not permitted to be published in Europe until 1501 AD., when Aldus Manutins printed the first Latin edition; and it was not until 1680 that Charles Blount made the first English translation of the first two of the eight manuscripts written by Philostratus.

Blount's notes on what he translated raised such a storm, that in 1693 the translation was condemned by the church and further publication prohibited.

Concerning the effects of Blount's translation, F. A. Campbell wrote:

"Fierce passions were let loose. Sermons, pamphlets, and volumes descended upon Blount like fireballs and hailstones, and his adversaries did not rest until the church had forbidden him to publish the remaining six manuscripts."

So excited was the priesthood by the translation into the modern tongues of Europe of the "Life of Apollonius", that it cast discretion to the wind and floundered into the very bog from which it was their chief aim to escape.

All that Blount said in his notes was to point out that we must admit the truth of the apparent miracles of Apollonius as well as those of the gospel Jesus, or, if the former were false, there was less ground to believe in the latter.

It was not until 1809 that Edward Berwick made the first complete English translation of the "Life of Apollonius." The church burnt the books so fast that in 1907 two London book shops of world-wide reputation searched and advertised in vain for a copy.

Modern encyclopedias give Apollonius but a short paragraph, stating that--

"The narratives of his work are so full of the miraculous, that many have regarded him as an imaginary character. The work of Philostratus, composed at the instance of Julia, wife of Severus, is generally regarded as a religious work of fiction" (Ency. Brit. vol. 1-2, p. 188).

Thus are we deceived by our histories and our encyclopedias.

The Christians know that ancient histories contain numerous accounts of Apollonius and his work but they do not so much as mention the name of the gospel Jesus.

Apollonius did much of his preaching and teaching in Ephesus, and there he was last seen on earth.

To make more certain the destruction of his writings, and of all memory and trace of Apollonius in and around Ephesus, history states that "None of the ancient cities have been so completely destroyed as was Ephesus."

That is more evidence to show how greatly the church feared the work and memory of the man whose life was used as that of the gospel Jesus, and whose writings it used as the Pauline Epistles and the Book of Revelation.

In his "Candid Words to the Christians," Hierocles declared that the history of Apollonius was the original of the stories of the gospel Jesus which, with the epistles and other writings of Apollonius (reinterpreting yet older writings), formed the basis of the Christian (Kristosite) scriptures that were used to make the New Testament.

This bold charge by Hierocles showed that the fraudulent work of the church fathers had been discovered, and caused them to see the urgent need of using every means at their command to conceal their fraud.

So the writings of Hierocles were destroyed by Lusebius, and all we know of them appears in the reply of Eusebius to the charge, from which one can judge the nature of the accusations Hierocles made.

Spiritual Vision

Apollonius displayed the activity of the sixth and seventh sense powers and the faculty of spiritual vision while preaching at Ephesus, when the Roman tyrant Domitian was assassinated and saw the deed done.

At first his voice dropped as if were terrified. Then, with less vigor, he continued to preach as one who, between statements, saw glimpses of something foreign to his subject. Finally he lapsed into silence, as one interrupted in his discourse.

Staring at the ground, he unconsciously advanced a few paces from his pulpit, and cried: "Courage, Stephanus; smite the tyrant," not as one who derives from a mirror a faint image of the event, but as one who sees it with his own eyes.

Then after a short pause, he continued: "Rejoice, my friends, for the tyrant dies this day. Yea, the very moment in which I was silent, he paid for his crimes. He dies."

The announcement was later confirmed by a messenger from Rome.

At another time, while sailing up the Nile from Alexandria to the very confines of Ethiopia, they met a bark steered by a youth named Timaison.

Apollonius asked the boy to give some account of his life, but Timaison blushed and said nothing. Then Apollonius, by the power of his sixth and seventh sense faculties, told his disciples the whole life history of the boy.

The youth, greatly amazed, confessed that it was true.

Chapter 4

CONSTANTINE THE GREAT

From Julius Caesar down to Constantine, the Romans had permitted the conquered countries to follow their religions and worship their gods.

This course continued until the time came when the discordant religicus waves of the east and the west met with a riot at Rome.

The bishops of the Kristosites (so-called Christians) of the east became worried by the increasing waves of doubt that flowed in upon their teachings from the Hesusites of the west.

By the end of the year 324 AD the conflict and confusion had become so intense and dangerous that something had to be done for the good of the Empire.

When Constantine had gained the throne of the Caesars, this was the religious state of his Empire. He saw that he had to take vigorous action to bring a more stable peace to his subjects in order to make his vast Empire safer.

The correct details of this strife and struggle have not been permitted to come down to us. They have been kept out of history books and encyclopedias. They were well known at the time, and were explained in the writings of Eunomius. That is the reason why his writings were not only destroyed, but also those of the Christian writers who attempted to answer him.

Two hundred long years after the Nicene convention, which we shall soon describe, the church so greatly feared the light of truth, that it would not afford to have the knowledge of Eunomius even remotely known. So by decree, the priestly rulers of Rome, ever the cowards of light, sought to destroy forever all trace of the terrible secret revealed in his writings.

That damaging evidence was the fact that the Roman Catholic Church is a monstrous sacerdotal fraud, a blighting bequest of the Roman Empire to the world, invented in a politico-religious convention, and forced upon the people by the combined power of the political and priestly rulers of that mighty nation.

When politics and religion are joined, the object is greater control of the masses.

Those selfish servants of fraud did not dream that truth cannot be concealed forever, and that in spite of their efforts to hide their fraudulent work and silence all opposition, the time would come when archeologists would dig from ancient ruins that evidence which would expose their black villainy to the eyes of an amazed world.

Justice may slumber long, but it always awakes, and retribution follows.

Truth may be buried ever so deeply beneath the ruins and dust

of the ages, but the time always comes when its penetrating light
bursts forth with resistless power, striking terror to the hearts
of its enemies and oppressors.

The real controversy which the Council of Nicea sought to settle,
was whether the Hindu Kristos of the east should prevail over the
Druidic Hesus of the west, or both be recognized and worshipped
accordingly.

That is the secret reason why no record was kept of the dark
proceedings and fierce debates of that first and most memorable
Christian council.

It has ever been a puzzle to Christian authors and critics why
no public record was preserved of the details and action of that
council.

It is certain that such a record was made; but for good reasons
the church never allowed the light of day to strike it. In the
musty vaults of the Vatican, along with other forbidden records of
ancient religions, it sleeps in quiet repose.

First Council of Nicea

Constantine first tried the policy of conciliating the subjects
of the western provinces by adopting their god Hesus as well as the
god Kristos of the east.

That policy failed and the controversy grew so dangerous between
the religious factions, that Constantine was constrained to summon
the leaders of the various sects to meet in council at Nicea, where
and when he would submit for consideration his pet scheme of adopting
the gods of both the eastern and western sects, uniting them in one
god to be known as Hesus Kristos, and the new god to take the place
and combine the characteristics of both gods.

The Great Religious Council, called by Constantine was convened
at the city of Nicea, in the Roman province of Bithyania, a country
in Asia Minor. It was considered safer for the scheme not to have
the convention anywhere near Rome, nor to have the people know anything of its real purpose.

Socrates Scholasticus says that the council was convened on the
20th day of May, A.D. 325, and it seems to have been terminated on
August 25th; but some say the struggle was so fierce that it lasted
into September.

We are told that some 1800 bishops were present, and Sabinus,
bishop of Heraclea, stated in a letter to a friend that, with the
exception of Constantine and Eusebius, the 300 bishops who finally
voted to support the motion to join the names of the two gods were
"a set of illiterate, simple creatures, who understood nothing much,"
to quote his words.

And it was by these ignorant prelates, subject to every kind of
motive, such as fear of being called heretics, desire to agree with
the powerful Emperor and win his favor, anxiety to bring the lengthy
proceedings to a close, who, simply by their votes, decided under

duress on the name of the New God who would represent the New Religion (Rhys, p.67).

Eusebius Pamphilus, of Caesarea, the first and principal orator at the council, had the first seat on the right hand, and in the name of the whole synod addressed Constantine, who sat in a golden chair.

Upon the formulation then and there of the Christian creed, which up to that day had no existence whatsoever, the whole work of Christiandom from that time on, was to destroy, to conceal, to oppose, everything which did not agree with that false, impious, and infamous sacerdotal prescription, engen ered in falsehood, sustained by fraud, and propagated by lies.

There was no alternative. It meant death to refuse to embrace that Christian creed.

Under the vigorous leadership of Eusebius, ably assisted by Athanasius, who was made bishop of Alexandria the following year for his strong support of Constantine's scheme, the assembled bishops, after a fierce and bitter debate, finally voted to adopt Constantine's scheme.

Of the 1800 bishops present, only 300 supported the fraud on the first vote. This made Constantine and Eusebius furious.

The leader of the opposition was one Arius. His faction drew up a declaration of their objections and presented it to the Council. As it opposed Constantine's scheme, his supporters promptly tore it to pieces, and declared it to be spurious and false.

So great was the uproar raised in this "holy" Christian convention, and so bitter and black were the reproaches cast upon the Arian faction, that Constantine had to call his Roman guards to restore any semblance of order.

Then with the support of Constantine and his armed guards, his faction all stood up and excommunicated Arius and all his followers on the spot. They were ordered from the meeting, and marched from the hall by the armed guards. Then by edict of Constantine, Arius was sent into exile.

This trick is as old as man, and has ruled all conventions and always will. Concentration camps in Europe and Asia have always been filled with political and religious prisoners. Small minorities in conventions create our governmental and religious systems. The people have no choice but to accept what these minority groups invent.

After Arius and his 1500 followers had been driven from the convention, Constantine's scheme was again presented to the 300 bishops who supported it in the first instant, and it was given unanimous support.

And that is the way the Christian world got its Christ Jesus, the savior of mankind who "washed us from our sins in his own blood" (Rev. 1:5).

Thus was instituted the wholesale destruction of all literature that bore upon the subjects of theology and history from the earliest times down to 325 AD.

The fragmentary manner in which any part of the literature of that period has been permitted to come down to us shows, that it must have contained much that was inconsistent with and damaging to the Christian cause; and the church, from the time of Constantine until the 16th century, monopolized the literature of the world, both sacred and profane.

It is this concatenation of corrupted and falsified ancient literature that is piously called by the church, "The Holy Scriptures of our Lord and Savior Jesus Christ."

Falsification

In line with the regular practice of the church, the subject of the Arius controversy was falsified in Christian history, as well as all other facts that expose the frauds of the church.

According to such history of this controversy as the church fathers have prepared for us, "this impious opinion of Arius should be anathematized, with all the blasphemous expressions he has uttered, in affirming that--

"The son of God (Jesus Christ) sprang from nothing, and that there was a time when he was not; saying, moreover, that the son of God was possessed of free-will, so as to be capable either of vice or virtue; and call him a creature and a work."--Dead Dudley, p.73.

Very clever; very deceptive and misleading. The facts are, that the Arian and Athanasian controversy was a fight over the combining of the names Hesus and Kristos. These facts do not appear in the history that Christianity has permitted to survive.

"This impious man" (Arius), says Christian history, "having thus been expelled from the church (with 1500 of his followers), a confession of faith, which is received to this day, was drawn up by unanimous consent; and, as soon as it was signed, the Council was dissolved" (Dudley).

"Most of the bishops who signed," says one writer, "did not consent to it in sincerity, but only in appearance." They had seen what happened to Arius and his followers, and had no desire to suffer a similar fate. So they signed and went home.

Caracalla, bishop of Nicomedia, privately declared that he did not believe there were half a dozen bishops present who believed in the doctrines and dogmas there formulated. He said that it was then and there agreed among the bishops who signed the creed, to destroy all writings that threw any light upon the fraudulent origin of Christianity. But the writings were not destroyed. They are in the dusty, moldy files of the Vatican at Rome.

Constantine solemnly confirmed the Nicene Creed as soon as it was signed, and he threatened with exile all who would not subscribe to it.

At the conclusion of the council, he raised all decrees of the assembly to the status of Laws of the Empire; declared them to be "divinely inspired"; and in several edicts, still partially extant, he commanded that they should be most faithfully observed by all his subjects (Dudley, pp.107).

Thus was born the Jesus Christ of the N. T. Thus was produced, by "unanimous consent," that "confession of Christian faith which is received to this day." Thus was perpetrated one of the most colossal frauds and deceptions in the annals of history. Thus did Constantine force Christianity upon the world.

The promoters of Christianity were careful to destroy everything relating to the Druidical and Hindu religions, and their gods Hesus and Kristos; while every effort was made by succeeding popes and emperors, after Constantine, to destroy all evidence as to the origin of Christianity and its Jesus Christ.

Dr. Westcott calls the first three centuries the "dark age of Christian literature," so scant are its remains. The facts are, there was no such literature.

During the dark ages, when the church was in power, research workers in the ruins of the past had to contend with serious opposition of the priesthood in everything that would throw any light on the origin of Christianity and its Jesus Christ. If they found anything, they did not dare to publish it on penalty of death.

When it became safe to do so, Rabbi Wise went to Jerusalem for the purpose of learning whether the gospel account of Christ's trial before Pilate was true. The learned doctor searched thru the old records of Pilate's court, which are preserved by the state authorities, for the trial of Jesus, but found nothing about it on record.

This is the manner in which Kristosism became Catholicism to settle a dangerous religious dispute.

The wars in those days had for their chief object the establishment of one religion over another. Religious hatred was bitter and intense. We get an illustration of this in modern political wars. It's all the same, whether religion or politics.

This is the revelation of the mystery that has puzzled the world for 1600 years. This is the secret story of the fraudulent manner in which the gospel Jesus came into being so long after the scriptures were written that were used to compile the N. T., that the name had to be interpolated wherever it appears; while the four gospels did not appear in their present form until after the 4th century. Even then the fraudulent scheme of revising the gospels continued until it was ended by the art of printing.

The name Jesus Christ unknown until after the Nicene council in 325. It appeared in no writings until that time. Farrer, in his life of Christ, is forced to concede and deplore the dearth of evidence as to the subject of his pen. He observes:

"It is little short of amazing that neither history nor tradition should have embalmed for us one certain or precious saying or circum-
-23-

stance in the life of the Savior of mankind, except the comparatively few events recorded in the four very brief biographies."

Jesus was habitually called "Jesus of Nazareth," according to the gospels. This leaves the impression that Nazareth of Galilee was the home of Jesus. The synoptic gospels represent that thirty years of his life were spent there. But according to history, there was no city nor village of Nazareth in that age. The Encyclopedia Biblica, written by theologians, the best biblical reference work in the English language, states:

"We cannot perhaps venture to assert positively that there was a city of Nazareth in the time of Jesus."

The compilers of the gospels did not know their geography and were strangers to the land about which they wrote. The fourth gospel says that Bethsaida was in Galilee (Jn. 12:21). According to history, there was no such town in that district and never was. Bethsaida was on the east side of the sea of Tiberias, whereas Galilee was on the west side of that sea.

According to the gospels, John was born at Bethsaida; but the fourth gospel shows that he doesn't know the geographical location of his own birth-place.

The Greeks changed the name Kristos to Christos, and the Romans changed the name Hesus to Jesus, while the English changed Christos to Christ.

Behind the falsified canonical accounts of the gospel Jesus Christ lies a lurid background of history in which such accounts are cleverly designed to conceal and distort.

Those who confine their research to the N. T. and to such history as the Christians have prepared for the public, cannot be expected to understand the peculiar conditions and antecedents that gave to the world Christianity and its Jesus Christ.

Furthermore, true history is seldom found. That is especially so with reference, to any account of the religious world prepared by Christians. No dependence can be put in any of it. For it is all designed to mislead and deceive.

Chapter 5

HESUS KRISTOS

In the religion that came from the east, the most prominent god was Krishna, Kristos, Cristos, Christos.

Apollonius spent some years in India studying the scriptures of their god, and took copies of these back with him when he returned to Antioch, where he came regarded as "an eloquent man, and mighty in the scriptures" (Acts 18:24), and where he taught the doctrines of the Hindu god.

In the religion of the Druids to the west of Rome, the leading god was known as Hesus, or Hesous, or Iseous, a word which, traced to its source, came from "Nous," meaning Mind or Intelligence, first of the Eons, beginning of all things, first revelation of the Divinity, or "Only Begotten" (Pike, p.560).

The Celtic Druids, wrote Godfrey Higgins, "were the priests of oriental colonies who emigrated from India." They were "the builders of stonehenge or Carnac, and of other Cycopean works, in Asia and Europe."

Kristos is a name derived from Kris, meaning the orb of the Sun. Krishna or Kristos was the Hindu Son God. In the ceremonies of the Indian Mysteries, Kristos was the incarnate spirit of the Hindu God Brahm, who in the course of time became the Chaldean Ab-Ram of the Jewish scriptures (Gen. 11:27), the same signifying Father Brahm or Father God.

The Druidical ceremonies came from India; and the Druids were originally Buddhists. They worshipped the Sun (Kris) under the name of Hesus.

Apollonius is mentioned in the Bible as Apollos, "an eloquent man, and mighty in the scriptures (Acts 18:24). The statement that he was a Jew, born at Alexandria, is another falsehood used to conceal his real identity. As he was destined to become the Jesus of the Bible because of his extraordinary work in religion, his true identity was carefully concealed.

Apollonius brought the Hindu religion into the Roman provinces to the east of Rome. He was known also by a name that meant the Son of Apollo--Apollo in turn meaning the Sun, the same as Kris.

The name Apollo means the same as Sol, Saul (Acts 7:58), and was frequently abbreviated into Pol, Paul, Polos, Paulus. He is the Paul of the Bible.

In the Acts, these names are changed in the spelling to suit the purpose of the author, and to conceal the fact that they were of the same meaning, and related to Apollonius, the greatest propagator of the Hindu religion in Rome in the first century AD; and beyond all question the author, expounder, and advocate of the Hindu theology set forth in the New Testament, no part of which ever had the remotest relation to any Jew or Hebrew theology.

So careful were the politico-religious founders of orthodox Christianity to conceal everything relating to Hesus of the Druids, that little mention of him can be found, and that little is contained in that valuable book, "The Celtic Druids," by Godfrey Higgins (London, 1826) Under the head, "The Druids Adored the Cross," he wrote:

"Having shown that the Cross was in common use in all religions long before the time of Christ, by the continental nations of the world, it is only necessary now to show that it was equally in use by the Celtic Druids in Britain and Ireland, in order to overthrow the arguments used to show certain monuments as being of Christian origin from the circumstances alone of their bearing the figure of a Cross.

"Shedius, in his treatise "De Mor. Germ." 24, speaking of the
Druids, confirms all I have said on this head. He wrote that the
Druids seek studiously for an oak tree, large and handsome, growing
up with two principal arms, in the form of a Cross, beside the main
stem upright. If the two horizontal arms are not sufficiently
adapted to the figure, they fasten a cross-beam to it.

"This tree they consecrate in this manner: Upon the right branch
they cut in the bark the word, Hesus; upon the center or upright
stem, the word, Taramis; upon the left branch, Belenus; over this,
above the going off of the arms, they cut the name of God, Thau
(the Mark of Ezek. 9:4); under all, the same repeated Thau.

"This tree so inscribed, they make their kebla, in the grove
cathedral, or summer church, toward which they direct their faces in
the offices of religion, as to the amber stone or the cove in the
temple of Abury; like as the Christians do to any symbol or picture
at the Altar" (Antiquity Unveiled, p.372).

When the church fathers made this discovery, they interpolated in
Deut. 21:23, "For he that is hanged (on a tree) is accursed of God,"
then interpolated in Gal. 3:13, "For it is written, Cursed is every
one that hangeth on a tree."

Here the evidence is preserved and rendered plain that the Druids
of Gaul, Germany, Britain, Ireland and Scandinavia had a trinity,
of which Thau (Thoth of the pre-Egyptians) was the supreme God,
Hesus the human executor of the will of the first, and Belenus, the
solar light and heat thru which all life was believed to have originated and to be preserved.

These were the three personifications of the Trinity. Hesus in
the trinity occupied the same position and represented the same
theological function as the Kristos of the Hindu trinity.

Furthermore, the Druidic Hesus was connected with and attached
to a natural, not an artificial, Cross, and that much nearer were
the Druids to the worship of the true God, the God of Nature, than
the Christian idolators who bow in adoration before the carved
crucifix.

According to tradition, the Druidic Hesus and the Hindu scriptures
reached Marseilles about 800 BC, being taken there by the Phoenicians,
who visited and traded in that region, and carried their religion
with them. The name of their god, Hesus, was derived from the word
Hes, meaning fire, fire-god, or sun-god, the Son of God.

The doctrines of Hesusism were propagated among the nations west
of Rome. It was not until 1500 years later, about 700 AD, that
Kristosism was introduced there by the Christian priesthood, and
then it was resisted even by resort to arms.

Hesusism had gained great ascendency and had some of the finest
schools in Gaul, Germany, Britain, and Ireland, and it was ardently
taught by St. Patrick and others.

The group that appropriated the Druidic god Hesus under the name
of Hesus Christos, sought diligently to conceal the facts by de-

stroying the evidence as to the source of their spurious deity Jesus
Christ.

Chapter 8

NEW TESTAMENT

After the Nicene Council had established the Roman Catholic
Church and invented its god, Hesus Kristos (Jesus Christ), suitable
literature to support the new religion and its new god was urgently
needed.

So Eusebius went into action, and collected such writings as
were available that could be revised, distorted and made to fit into
the Christian scheme. These writings were those of Apollonius.

There is much mystery as to how the writings of this extraordinary
teacher became available for use in the Christian scheme. It was
due to the sly plagiarism of one Marcion (Marcus, Phil. 1:24), the
Mark of the second gospel, a native of Cappadocia, the country of
Apollonius.

Apollonius, the greatest oracle and philosopher of the Roman
Empire, never made public his translations of the Hindu scriptures
received by him while in India. He wrote them in the Samaritan
tongue, and they were not available to Greek and Latin scholars of
the time.

The great city of Antioch, built about 300 BC, was the capital
of the Greek kingdom of Syria, and long the chief city of Asia Minor.
Here Apollonius spent much time preaching the gospel of Chrishna,
the Hindu savior. This is how the N. T. composers in 325 AD told
the story:

"Then departed Barnabas (real name Damis, disciple of Apollonius)
to Tarsus, for to seek Saul (Apollonius); and when he found him, he
brought him into Antioch. And it came to pass, that a whole year
they assembled themselves with the church, and taught much people.
And the disciples were called Christians first in Antioch" (Acts
11:25,26).

Marcion was a scholar and a thinker. He was an influential
Cappadocian, whose native tongue was the Samaritan. He went to
Antioch after the great Apollonius had been dead about twenty years,
and there found his valuable manuscripts, which Apollonius had never
made public. Being an educated man, Marcion saw that the writings
contained rare secrets of Nature and Creation unknown to the world
at large, and he regarded this a grand opportunity to become great
at the expense of another man, now dead.

So Marcion secretly appropriated the writings of Apollonius, and
altered and interpolated them to suit this purpose, and thus became
the actual Father of the New Testament.

To conceal the source of the writings, and to hide his own
identity, Marcion interpolated that description of Paul (Apollonius)
which was later copied by Lucian (Luke). He translated the writings
into Greek and Latin, with both of which he was as familiar as with

his own, then took them to Rome and introduced them to public notice for his own benefit and aggrandizement. This happened somewhere between 130 and 150 AD.

Of course the names of Jesus, Jesus Christ, or Jesus the Christ did not appear in these writings until later inserted therein by Eusebius and his assistants after 324 AD. Before that, in those writings, which originally came from India, appeared the name of the Hindu god and savior, Chrishna.

It is a matter of history that the people of the Antioch area worshipped Christos, the Hindu Savior, and sang hymns to him. Pliny wrote about the people "singing hymns to Christos."

This Chrishna became Christ, and the Christosites became Christians. The change in the words was so slight as to attract no unusual attention. That easily was the terrible fraud perpetrated by the priesthood.

Hormisdas admitted that as late as 525 AD the writings of Marcion were still in existence; that they were copies of the writings of Apollonius, and that he helped to destroy them.

Charles B. Waite, in his "History of the Christian Religion to AD 200", showed beyond all question of doubt that the author of Marcion's gospel, the Mark, Luke and Pauline Epistles, was one and the same person. He declared that from these writings, the New Testament was fabricated by Christian plagiarists.

Some of Marcion's writings appear in the present Mark gospel, in which there is no reference to the virgin birth, and Christ (Chrishna) appears only as a singularly gifted magician. The last twelve verses of the last chapter of this gospel were added by Eusebius and his assistants, or at a later time.

The Matthew which, in its original form, was copied from the Mark, said nothing unusual about the birth of Christ. The first two chapters are an afterthought. This gospel originally began with the 3rd chapter, in a tone similar to the Mark. Eusebius and his helpers prefaced it with one of the two genealogies of Jesus. Then they added a short account of how Jesus was born (1:18-25). Lastly, they added the legends of chapter 2, which was copied from those of Chrishna.

It is not known who wrote the Matthew, nor when the work was accredited to Matthew. In its original form it was headed as the work of Mathieuo, who was said to be the principle disciple of Deva Bodhistaous, a Buddist prophet. But Mathieuo was not the name of a man. It is a compound word that means the following: "Ma" means spirit as it exists in the body; "thieu" is analogous to the Greek "theus"; and "O" is the eternal Circle that symbolized God in the ancient religion. The word Mathieuo means the Spirit of God working in a circle.

The church fathers changed Mathieuo to Matthew, then made it falsely appear that this was a man Jesus saw sitting at the receipt of custom; "and he saith unto him, Follow me. And he arose, and followed him" (Mat. 9:9).

-28-

Lucian, a Greek scholar and satirist, wrote the Luke gospel, but not as it appears in the N.T.

Lucian wrote a fable, and said so. He did not weave it around the gospel Jesus. For in his day this mythical character was unknown.

When Lucian addressed his epistle to Theophilus, to tell him "the certainty of those things, wherein thou hast been instructed," he had in mind had been preached by the greatest philosopher and theologian of the first century--Apollonius of Tyana.

Demas was the beloved disciple of Apollonius, and is mentioned in Col. 3:13, and Philemon 1:24. Lucius of Cyrene (Acts 13:1), was his secretary.

To him Demas dictated a long account of his Master's life, travels and teachings, which Lucius transcribed. He also helped Demas write practically all of the epistles of the N.T.

Lucius Apuleius, a philosopher and follower of Lucian, stated that in his day the belief was general that Apollonius was a reincarnation of Gautama Buddha, and that special efforts were made by the followers of Apollonius to promulgate his teachings, as they contained all that scholars considered good and useful in all religions and philosophies, then known. Their purpose was to promulgate a religion of peace among men, and their course was ably followed by Potamon, Ammonius Saccas, Plotinus, and others. He said that the mythical gods of his day, such as Jupiter, Orpheus, Apollo, etc., were but substitutes for Hesus, Chrishna, Buddha, Osiris, etc.

Apuleius furnishes the key that unlocks the mysteries that attended what has been called the "Christianity" of the first three centuries of this era. It was the effort made by the followers of Apollonius to spread his teachings, as they contained all they considered good and useful in all religions and philosophies then known. And his teachings were based on those of the Hindu Masters as contained in their "Code of the Initiated."

It is a revelation to learn that Apollonius was regarded as a reincarnation of Gautama Buddha. This discloses the secret of his visit to the Masters in the "Mountains of the Wise," and the distinguished honors conferred upon him by the Buddhist Masters.

This is the remarkable man whose extraordinary teachings Lucian had in mind when he addressed to Theophilus his epistle which was destined to become the third gospel of the N.T. To him, Apollonius was known as Apollos in the Greek tongue, and as Paulus in the Roman; and it was understood by all scholars of the time, that he was relating, in fabulous form, the life, travels and miracles of Apollonius.

Lucian knew that many of his statements were not factual truths, and admitted it. But that made little difference to him, for he was engaged in writing a fable to make even greater the great work of a great man.

We do that today in the case of George Washington, Abraham Lincoln, and our other heroes.

-29-

Like dramatic and poetic authors, he exaggerated and used events that suited his purpose, such as raising the dead, etc., regardless of whether true or false. For those who could not raise the dead were not gods.

Lucian attempted to justify his work by asserting that all men are selfish, so far as securing the necessities and comforts of life are concerned, and in gaining prominence over their fellowman. That has been done in all ages, and always will be. "In fact," said he, "that is not so bad a quality of human nature as some might imagine. To attain prosperity and avoid adversity is a necessary incentive to human effort." He was a practical man.

Lucian further said that, by comparing notes with Grecian, Roman, Samaritan and other authors, it was found that one and the same fable ran through the religious systems of all nations--as to their gods being born of virgins. The idea became so prevalent that laws were enacted to the effect that death would be imposed upon women who claimed to have been overshadowed or impregnated by God or the gods. So Lucian followed the regular path of other authors and made his god the son of a virgin.

Gods and virgin mothers, divine sons and stable births, persecuting monarchs, angelic annunciations and foster-fathers, appear in the scriptures of all ancient religions. There are scores of legends of the miraculous birth of gods, demi-gods, and heroes in the ancient world. It was so common as to be a prerequisite condition to bring the hero within the scope of the god realm.

When Lucian wove his fable around a mythical god, he believed rational men were sufficiently intelligent to know that he was relating a fabulous tale and not a factual one. He did not pretend to be writing the "word" of God, but was simply relating an allegory to attract public attention.

Nor can we blame him because we are such suckers as to swallow his fable as the "word" of God, and upon it base our hope of a future life.

Long after he was dead, the scheming forgers distorted his fable and interpolated the name of their mythical god in the place of his, then took the sword in one hand and his fable in the other, and to the people said, Swallow this dose as the "word" of God--or die!

The fables of all gods are the same. That of Chrishna resembles that of the gospel Christ so exactly, that an early Christian missionary, to India was astounded to make this discovery, and expressed the opinion that most parts of the Chrishna and Christ legends came from a common source. That is absolutely correct.

The tragedy comes when the church and state join hands and, on penalty of death, make their subjects and slaves swallow as factual truth these ancient fables, traditions and legends of these mythical gods. Then the church authorities scare these subjects and slaves into believing these fables by publishing such wild statements as that of the Bishop of Manchester, England, who wrote:

"The very foundation of our faith, the very basis of our hopes, the very dearest of our consolations are taken from us, when one line of that sacred volume (bible), on which we base everything, is shown to be untruthful and untrustworthy" (Bible Myths, p.17).

The first three books of the N. T. are called the synoptic gospels because so closely related in language. Much of their language is almost identical, regardless of their contradictions, showing that they are largely copied from the same document.

The Mark is the shortest, the simplest, and the oldest of the four. It has no prologue, like the John, no preface, like the Luke, and no story of the infancy, as have the Matthew and the Luke.

"It is impossible to pass from the synoptic gospels," writes the Rev. B.F. Westcott, "to the fourth without feeling that the transition involves the passage from one world of thought to another. No familiarity with the general teachings of the gospels, no wide conception of the character of Jesus, is sufficient to destroy the great contrast that exists in form and spirit between the fourth and the three preceding gospels."

When the forging compilers of the N.T. said that the 4th gospel and the Revelation were written by the same man, they had the evidence to prove this to be a fact. But they knew they were lying when they said that man was John, the disciple whom Jesus loved (Jn.20:2).

The fourth gospel and the Revelation are the work of a scholar, a philosopher, a Master; whereas both Peter and John are definitely described as "unlearned and ignorant men" (Acts 4:13). This fact is confirmed by the statement that they were "fishers" (Mar.4:18,21). Such men are not noted for learning and wisdom; otherwise they would not be "fishers."

The internal evidence of the gospel itself is conclusive against the theory that John wrote it. Some of the most important events in the life of Jesus were witnessed by John, the synoptic gospels declare, yet the author of the John knows nothing about them and never mentions them.

The John gospel, the Revelation, and the Pauline Epistles, are the work of Apollonius himself. The first two named were prepared toward the close of his life, when his knowledge of Nature and the creative processes of the Universe was more ripened and mature. It is there that he relates allegorically the doctrines taught him by the Hindu Masters; while the allegories of the Revelation are drawn from every great religion of the ancient world. The drama there unfolded is synthetic and includes the profound teachings of the ages.

The same tone appears in the John and the Pauline Epistles, where Apollonius tells the world that God is spirit, and that it is the spirit that animates the flesh (Jn.6:63). He continues in the same vein: "Know ye not that ye are the temple of God, and that the Spirit of God dwelleth in you" (1 Cor. 3:16; 1 Cor. 6:19). Then he explains the difference between the natural and the spiritual body (1 Cor.15:44).

Lastly, he dimly refers to the great mystery of the Masters in the last eight verses of 1 Cor. 15:50-58. Then he says: "Flesh and blood cannot inherit the kingdom of God." Yet the Christian forgers make Job say, "In my flesh shall I see God" (Job 19:26), a falsification necessary to support the physical resurrection of Jesus.

The entire John gospel has been badly interpolated and distorted. It contradicts the other gospels. It makes Moses and Aaron out as liars by declaring, "No man hath seen God at any time" (1:18). Moses talked to God face to face (Ex. 33:11; Deut. 5:4). This gospel evidently ended originally with the 11th chapter. From the 12th chapter on the story prepared the way for the end of the drama by the crucifixion. Until these chapters were added, the early church fathers declared the John was spurious, and had no place in the N.T. But that defect was remedied by the addition mentioned.

The whole fraudulent story of the mythical Jesus Christ is interpolated in the N.T. merely as a mosaic composed of differently colored bits of stone from the quarries of the older religions.

In those days, before the invention of the printing press, all books were hand-written, and he who wanted a copy of a book, hired a public scribe to write it for him (Mark. 2:6). It was then very easy for the priesthood or any one to interpolate in the scriptures anything desired, and that was done on a large scale as overwhelming evidence shows. In fact, one cannot believe anything in the so-called Word of God unless well supported by reliable evidence.

This fraudulent work was freely used all through the Old Testament, with interpolations here and there to make it appear the ancient scriptures predicted the coming of the gospel Jesus. A typical example of this fraud appears in the following interpolation:

"Behold, a virgin shall conceive, and bear a son, and shall call his name Immanuel" (Isa. 7:14).

All literature of the first three centuries AD had to pass thru the censorial hands of such Christian authorities as Pope Sylvester I, Eusebius, and their coadjutors and successors who, from the 4th century to the time the art of printing ended it, were assiduously engaged in interpolating, distorting, forging, mutilating and destroying all traces of evidence within their reach, that might reveal the true origin and nature of Christianity.

Consternation reigned in the Christian camp when the art of printing was invented. That would end the altering and distorting of biblical passages.

In the year 1444 Caxton published the first book ever printed in England; and in 1474 the then bishop of London, in a convocation of his clergy, said, "If we do not destroy this dangerous invention, it will one day destroy us" (Biblical Myths, p.438).

Due to the concealment of Marcion and the Christian writers who followed him, nowhere in the N.T. appears one definite reference to Apollonius, if we except a few verses reading, "For while one saith, I am of Paul; another, I am of Apollos. Who then is Paul, and who is Apollos, but ministers by whom ye believed" (1 Cor. 3:4,5).

The studied avoidance of the compilers of the N.T. to mention

Apollonius definitely, is proof that his recognition by Christian authors would be fatal to their scheme.

The first Christian writer to mention Apollonius by that name, is Origen, in his work against Celsus.

Apollonius had been dead nearly a hundred years when Celsus wrote a work called "The True Word" against Christianity, which mentioned Apollonius as a great philosopher, oracle, and magician, and which work was destroyed by the Christian fathers. Origen claims to give quotations from it.

Dr. Lardner admits that all thru the 3rd century, frequent mention was made of the name and teachings of Apollonius. But it was not until Hierocles, in the 5th century, boldly charged upon the Christian priesthood their plagiarism of the writings of Apollonius, that the priesthood resorted to every conceivable means to conceal the truth which Hierocles proclaimed with such portentous force.

Hierocles was an author of note and enjoyed a great reputation. For his truthful charge against the priesthood, he was thrown in prison, cruelly flogged and threatened with death unless he recanted; and his writings were fiercely destroyed by the Christian fathers, who took extra care to see that the works of this formidable exponent of truth and opponent of Christian fraud did not survive to inform the people how basely they were deceived by the church.

After Greenly examines the New Testament and comments thereon, he summarized his findings as follows:

1. There is no external evidence of an historical Jesus. No historical Jesus is known to Paul. No historical Jesus is known to the authors of the Didache.

2. No historical episodes of action can be extracted from the gospels with any reliability. The "Nazareth" problem is extremely obscure, and it is doubted that such a village existed at the time.

3. The Twelve Apostles are unknown to Paul, and are clearly mythical in the gospels. An ethic deriving from an historical Jesus is unknown to Paul, and in the gospels is either late or of external origin.

4. A definite Christian teaching eludes us in the gospels. The style of the Gospel Jesus is not that of a real and living person. The closing scenes, when scrutinized, break down as history. They are interpretable as drama, and only as drama.

5. Parallels to every salient episode of the gospels are disclosed by Comparative Mythology.

6. Various scattered clues indicate a real development behind that which appears upon the face of the gospels.

Dr. Greenly didn't know the half of it. He saw almost nothing of the "real development" contained and concealed in the gospel parables.

-33-

It is known now that the N.T. is the work of the priesthood. It was written, compiled and perpetuated by and for the priesthood, to fulfill the "prophecy" that "Ye shall be unto me a kingdom of priests" (Ex. 19:6).

Michaelis says that "no manuscript of the N.T. now extant is prior to the sixth century," and Dr. Hooykaas says: "The gospels can hardly be said to have authors at all. They had only editors or compilers. Then these works, from time to time, were distorted by introductory matter or interpolations from the hands of later persons" (Bible for Learners, p.29).

Rev. B.F. Westcott writes: "For hundreds of years the scriptures were in the hands of the clergy only, were all written by hand, and they had every opportunity to insert or change whatsoever they pleased; thus we find them distorted and full of interpolations."

As evidence of this distortion, in Mat. 11:19, it is said: "From the days of John the Baptist until now (as if that were a long time) the kingdom of heaven suffereth violence."

This statement contains evidence in itself to show that it was not written until years after the "days of John the Baptist"; yet in Mat. 3:13, we read: "Then cometh Jesus from Galilee to Jordan unto John, to be baptized of him,"as if that were but a few days off."

The general ignorance of those who wrote the four gospels as they now appear in the N. T.,not only of the geography and statistics of Judea, but even of its language--their egregious blunders, which no writers who had lived in that age could be conceived of as making, prove that the authors were not Jews, had never been in Palestine, and neither lived at nor at anywhere near the times of which their narratives seem to refer.

The early church fathers knew better than to place much reliance upon the genuineness and accuracy of the scriptures in their possession; while critics of every shade of opinion are agreed that many of the early Christian scriptures are, or contain, the deliberate forgeries of zealous monks who saw little harm in thus attempting to strengthen the cause they had at heart.

Fortunately for historical truth, older writings, stone tablets and monuments have been discovered and deciphered in recent years, which enable us to detect the alterations, interpolations and additions that the later scribes made to the N.T. Furthermore, the documents themselves contain internal evidence, such as unguarded references to later events, which show that they were written, as we have them, by those who lived much later in time than the reputed authors.

Critics show that by the 16th century there were no less than 1822 texts and versions of the N.T., all different. There were 129 N. T. uncials used by the different churches between the 4th and 8th centuries. These manuscripts were all different. Each of the 129 writers had altered God's "word" to make it say what they wanted it to say.

Man built bibles to deceive the masses and support his church.

Then he called it the "word" of God to intimidate the ignorant masses
and constrain them to support the church. The contents of the bible
were not altered and revised to make a record of facts, but to state
what the priesthood wanted it to state.

As late as 1800 Christendom believed the four gospels were composed independently of each other by different authors, in spite of
the fact that the first three of them agree verbatim, verse after
verse.

At the beginning of the 19th century the darkness began to lift,
and the true history of the N.T. began to unfold. It slowly seeped
into the more liberal minds that the four gospels were taken from
a common source, and were based on the legends of the ancient gods
and saviors.

Thus the archeologists are digging from the debris of the ages,
a damaging chapter of biblical history which the church fathers
supposed they had entirely obliterated forever from the records of
the world, so that no man would ever know that Christology is the
biggest fraud on earth.

"Every dogma of Christianity has been eaten away by the attrition
of the remorseless current of increasing knowledge."

Chapter 7

MORE EVIDENCE OF CHRISTIAN FRAUD

The evidence which proves that Christianity and its Jesus are
frauds is overwhelming.

We shall notice that of Euthalius, a Greek theologian of the
fifth century, who was a commentator on the so-called Pauline Epistles.

He said it was generally known in his day by the leaders of
Christianity, that the writings from which these epistles were compiled were brought from India by Apollonius, and that the John gospel
was written by Apollonius himself toward the close of his life, when
he retired to the isle of Patmos (Rev. 1:9), to end his days in
isolation from humanity, and that while there he also wrote the long
parable known as The Revelation.

The John gospel, according to Euthalius, was a blending with
what the inspired Seer hoped for, and the knowledge which he feared
to impart in such terms as uneducated men could understand.

The Acts of the Apostles, continued Euthalius, related to the
work of Apollonius and his disciples, and this fact was fully understood by the Gnostics and Neo-Platonists up to the time of Eusebius
of Caesarea.

Ammonius Saccas, Plotinus, Porphyry and their followers, according to Euthalius, were Gymnosophists, Gnostics and Neo-Platonists
combined. They were sincere teachers and philosophers, and had no
idea nor intention of promulgating anything but that which they regarded as facts and truth.

Their teachings had relation to the Brahmanical end Buddhistic canonical narratives concerning the Hindu savior Krishna, who was said to have been born 3670 BC, and was worshipped as an incarnation of Brahma, or the Spirit of the Universe. Brahmanism is Nature Worship.

The canonical epistles, according to Euthalius, were all derived from the writings of Apollonius, who, to conceal that fact, was called Saul, Pol, or Paul, or Paulus. The names Peter, John, James, and Jude, were added to the other epistles that were sent to communities too insignificant to be mentioned.

All of these writings of Apollonius, which were based on Brahmanical and Buddhistic Nature Worship, were appropriated by Eusebius to promote his Christian scheme, to do which he personified the symbols and literalized the allegories of the Hindu religion. But he died before he was able to complete the work, and Euthalius, regarding this as a grand opportunity to gain fame, finished the work Eusebius had begun.

Euthalius put the Hindu writings of Apollonius into the form he desired, and then eliminated from them all mention of Apollonius, Krishna, and Buddha, and substituted the names now contained in the Bible.

This fraudulent work of Eusebius and Euthalius became the better assured in proportion as the original writings and all traces of them were destroyed. However, they were not destroyed, but were concealed in the library of the Vatican.

According to Euthalius, the gospel according to Matthew embodied the Phoenician idea of a god-savior.

The original name affixed to this gospel was Mathieous. "Ma" meant spirit as it exists in the human form; "thieu" is analogous to the Greek "theus" (god); and "O" is the eternal Circle which symbolizes God. The word Mathieuo meant the Spirit of God working in a circle.

These things were known to Dr. Georgius Faustus in the 16th century and were published by him. As a result, the priesthood charged that "he had sold himself to the devil," So when Goethe presented the salvation of Faust (Faustus), he went contra to the reports of the church, "which always made the damnation of Faust the legitimate result of his compact with the devil."

Here is the secret reason why the priesthood imprisoned him, confiscated his property, and suppressed his publication. In a World of Fraud it is always a serious crime to tell the Truth.

The Mathieuo gospel was originally written in the Syro-Chaldiac tongue, not in Greek as the priesthood claimed. The other three gospels, as they appear in the Greek, are equally copies of older originals in other languages. As they appear in Greek, they are the work of Marcion and Lucian, who were educated in Greek.

It was about AD 350 that Christian priesthood began the attempt to bring over the Armenian worshippers of the Hindu Kristos (Hesus

Kristos), by canonizing and adopting the Buddhistic-Armenian gospel of Mathieuo, changing the name to Matthew.

This gospel attempts to make it appear that this was the Matthew who was "sitting at the receipt of custom," and rose and followed Jesus (Mat. 9:9). More fraud.

The gospel of Matthew was written by Apollonius at an early period of his career, and the John near the close of his life, after he had matured his theological conceptions.

It is evident from his writings that the theological and philosophical theories of Apollonius changed as he advanced in his realization of the Spiritual Department of Natural Forces and Causes, and hence the more pronounced is the Spiritual Nature of his later writings as compared with the less spiritually developed characteristics of the first gospel.

There is a singular analogy between the name of Apollonius and John. They are both designations of the Light that lightest all men coming into the world, the Sun (Jn. 1:9).

Among the ancient Greeks, the Sun was alike designated Apollo and Ion (1 Cor. 3:5,6). ION is the Greek name of the Sun, etymologically speaking . "I" means One, and "ON" means Being--One Being, God.

The Ionic branch of the Greek race were "children of the Sun."

The word Freemason comes from the Egyptian Phree-Massen, which means "Son of Light."

Eusebius and his Christian successors, who labored so hard to conceal the source of Christianity and deprive Apollonius of the credit of his amazing work, substituted Ion or John for Apollonius.

Being an initiate of the Indian Mysteries and a student of their scriptures, Apollonius wove into his writings the theological and philosophical teachings of Brahmanism and Buddhism, the gods of which were Kristos (Greek-Christos) and Gautama Buddha, which gods are known in various other languages by still other names. But regardless of names or where found, they all go back to the Mysteries of India.

Euthalius completed the interpolation and distortion of the scriptures which Eusebius began. He acknowledged that he broke the Epistles and the Acts of the Apostles into chapters and verses, in order to add to, or omit from, the context of the writings. He collated them with the copies in the library of Eusebius Pamphilus at Caesarea, and was fully acquainted with the alterations that had been made from the originals by Eusebius.

Euthalius admitted that in his day the Hindu writings, as copied by Apollonius, were in the Pamphilian library at Caesarea, and that he modified them to suit his own theories, and eliminated the names of Apollonius, Buddha and Krishna, and substituted the name of Paul and the Jesus idea.

Chapter 8

THE MYSTIC SLEEP

Then they also which are fallen asleep in Christ are perished
(1 Cor. 15:18).

Just another distorted statement in the Bible.

Various references to "falling asleep" appear in the Bible. As
the ancient writings were distorted, when not destroyed, the layman
knows nothing of the "Mystic Sleep" taught by the Ancient Masters.

The Mystic Sleep parable appears in the 11th chapter of the John.
Being omitted from the other gospels, it may be the parable was unknown to their authors, otherwise they had mentioned it; for it is
the most amazing exhibition of supernatural power displayed by the
gospel Jesus.

The Cosmic Circle

In ancient symbolism, the vertical line of the Cosmic Cross
divides the Cosmic Circle into lateral halves, called male and fe-
male. The horizontal line divides the Circle into upper and lower
halves, called heaven and earth.

The Cosmic Generator (Osiris) rules the upper half (heaven),
while the Cosmic Generatrix (Isis) rules the lower half (earth).

In his descent from the upper half (heaven) to the lower half
(earth), man symbolically falls from his celestial state into a
terrestrial prison, the dense earthly body, the lower half of the
Circle.

The church, for profit and power, twisted the fable so it would
mean the actual fall of man into sin and the loss of his soul. (sol).

Man does not fall into sin, nor lose his soul (solar spark).

In the upper half (heaven) of the Circle, man is invisible Spirit
In the lower half (earth) he is vested, robed in a carnal body, thus
corresponding with his environment.

He now becomes "lost" in the physical world of change, on the
tempestuous "Sea of Illusion", across which he must sail (symbolically
to Mt. Ararat, the port where he sheds the "corruptible" (body) and
"puts on incorruption, and this mortal puts on immortality"(1 Cor.
15:53).

The Masters taught that birth in the physical world is the
descent of Spirit into Matter; and that death in the physical world
is Birth in the Spiritual World,--the Born Again process (Jn. 3:3,5),
the return to man's original status,-"statu quo ante physical birth."

Sense Powers

Man's Sense Powers are definitely Spiritual Powers. But as
Spiritual Man becomes robed in a physical body, he usually loses

-38-

his omnipotent, omnipresent, and omniscient Spiritual Sense Powers, and loses contact with the spiritual realm. In the change, he becomes equipped with limited sense powers that make him harmonize with his physical environment.

In this change, the memory of his antecedent spiritual life grows dim, and usually fades out entirely, leaving in its place, in some cases, that strange intuition of Immortality.

Antecedent Incarnations

Amazing cases are recorded of people who appear to have retained so much spiritual memory, or memory of their spiritual life, that they remember some events that occurred many centuries before.

Colonel Roches, of France, used hypnotism to take his subjects back thru what seemed to be a series of antecedent incarnations.

A. R. Martin, of Pennsylvania, claimed no psychic gift, but was able to take the seeker back thru antecedent experiences. He made a study of hypnotism, and became interested in the work of Dr. Cannon, who could send the subject's memory back to the moment of birth, but no farther.

In his book, "Researches into Reincarnation and Beyond," Martin recounted some fifty of his thousands of cases.

Not every subject could be sent back thru his preceding incarnations. The ability to relax physically and mentally is vital.

A certain orthodox minister visited Martin, and was sent back thru some of his previous incarnations. Some of the experiences caused him to burst into tears, and he asked whether it were conceivable that he had lived thru so much.

Martin replied, "If all that were not in your mind, it could not be coming out."

The preacher saw himself in the past as a ruler of a tenth century Chinese province. During this review he lectured on Buddhism, chanting in Chinese. Later he saw himself in a Swiss chalet as an old man, futilely trying to comfort a distraught daughter.

More amazing was the fact that in all these instances, his present physical body assumed, as if by magic, the posture, tone and bearing suitable to the character that he was in previous incarnations.

Once he appeared to suffer such agony from thirst, that a doctor present could hardly be restrained from administering to the "dying" man. But when he came out of the hypnotic trance, he did not want a drink.

Some psychologists hold that these visions of antecedent incarnations are caused by contact with Universal Mind father than by personal experience.

But Individual Mind is only a phase of Universal Mind, the former being limited in the physical body of man by his Sense Powers or by his State of Consciousness.

Man's knowledge of himself and his environment is limited by his State of Consciousness, which is limited by his Sense Powers, which are often quite faulty, and almost always below par.

Mind Power is potentially omnipotent, omnipresent, and omniscient. It may be increased to the point where man can see objects and hear sounds anywhere on earth, and even to the point where "there is nothing covered, that shall not be revealed; and nothing hid, that shall not be known" (Mat. 10:26).

Incarnation

The Masters fabulized Incarnation as death and burial of Spirit in Matter. They said, "The Soul becomes 'cribbed, cabined, and confined' in the limitations of the carnal body, as it loses a dimension of Consciousness at each step on the descending path. It becomes bound in the sensual and palpable, after previously having had the power to range at will throughout limitless space and Universal Thought."

According to the Masters, when the Spirit descends into its physical temple, on its approach and at the moment of its divulsion from its celestial abode, there ensues an intermediate or preparatory stage, a diminution of Consciousness, termed a swoon.

In the Tibetan Book of the Dead, a rare work which the church failed to find and destroy, the celestial body is represented as retrograding step by step into the lower state of Consciousness. Each step by step into the lower state of Consciousness. Each step downward to incarnation is preceded by a swooning into unconsciousness. This swooning on the descent, from the upper (heaven) to the lower (earth) part of the Circle, is comparable to falling asleep.

This is the ancient Mystic Sleep Fable from which the church fathers stole the story that Jesus was notified that Lazarus (Ausares) was sick.

Jesus said, "This sickness is not unto death" (Jn. 11:4).

According to the biblical account, an emergency call for help was sent to Jesus, but he calmly tarried "two days still in the same place" (Jn. 11:6).

Then Jesus said, "Lazarus (Ausares) sleepeth; but I go, that I may awake him out of (the Mystic) Sleep" (Jn. 11:11).

Since that story appeared in the Bible, the gullible masses have swallowed the fable as freely as children swallow the Santa Claus fable.

Ausares

When the neophyte was initiated in the Egyptian Mysteries, he was shown the figure of Ausares (Osiris) on its funeral bier. At the head stood Nephthys, and at the foot, Isis, the "two sisters of Lazarus," who weep for him. Hovering over the body, symbolizing the Soul, was "a dove with out-stretched wings" (Budge).

This scene was used to teach the neophyte how the celestial man looks down on the body of terrestrial man in its demise.

The New from the Old

Lazarus "had lain in the grave four days" (Jn. 11:17). That is the usual time required for grain to germinate and the new plant to appear.

That (seed) which thou sowest is not quickened, except it die (1 Cor. 15:36).

As the New rises from the old grain that is buried, so the New rises from the demised body of man.

Buried grain becomes not extinct. In the birth of the New, the material part of the grain disintegrates and returns to cosmic gas. The Life of the grain goes on.

In death, the demised body of man never rises from the grave in its organized form. Not even the body of the gospel Jesus. But the Life, the Spirit, goes on, to reappear in due course in another material body.

According to the Masters, the rule is that man must go thru seven incarnations in order to reach the state of Consciousness so perfect that Individual Spiritualization becomes complete and further incarnation is unnecessary.

Jesus said Lazarus was not dead but sleeping, and needed to be awakened.

Life in the grain is not dead but sleeping, and needs to be awakened by the process of germination, set in action by burial in the grave (ground) for four days, usually.

On the fourth day New Life appears. On the fourth day Lazarus was raised (Jn. 11:17).

Egyptian Drama

In the Egyptian drama, thousands of years before the Christian era, Horus raised his "dead" father Ausares (Osiris) at Anu, by calling unto him in the cave to rise and come forth.

Thousands of years later, Jesus "cried in a loud voice, Lazarus (Ausares) come forth" (Jn. 11:43).

When this Egyptian fable was literalized in the New Testament, Horus became Jesus, Ausares became Lazarus, and Anu became Bethany.

In the Egyptian drama, the two sisters, Isis and Nephthys, were present. In the gospel narrative they become Mary and Martha, "sisters of Lazarus."

The evidence shows that the church fathers culled the contents of the New Testament from many sources. The 11th chapter of the John was excerpted from the Egyptian Book of the Dead, which shows that five thousand years ago, the Egyptian God Ausares Osiris) said:

"I am the resurrection and the Life" (Budge). The church fathers put that statement in the mouth of their Jesus (Jn. 11:23).

He that believeth not these literalized fables in the Bible, shall be damned (Mk. 16:16).

The church fathers put that statement in their Bible, and then used it as their authority for murdering more than seventy million people for refusing to believe in the literalized fables in the Bible

Soul (Solar Body)

The symbolical sleep of the Soul (Solar Body) in the material body is the reign of physical man.

But there is no actual sleep of the Solar Body; it is only apparent. For the Life of the body is the activity of the Soul, and the functions of the body are the work of the Soul.

We must go back to the Zodiac and Astrology for the Masters' fable of the Soul, a term that means Solar Body

The Galaxy, says Macrobius, crosses the Zodiac in two opposite points, Cancer and Capricorn, the tropical points of the glorious Sun's course, ordinarily called the Gates of the Sun by the Masters.

These two tropics, before the time of Macrobius, corresponded with these Constellations, but, in his day, with Gemini and Sagittarius because of the Precession of the Equinoxes.

However, the signs of the Zodiac remained unchanged; and the Milky Way crossed at the signs Cancer and Capricorn, but not at those Constellations.

Cancer symbolized the Gate of Physical Birth. Thru this gate the Soul descended to Earth, and, at the death of the body, it re-ascended thru Capricorn to its Spiritual Home. The former gate was termed the Gate of Earth, and the latter the Gate of Heaven.

In its descent, until the Soul reached the sign of Cancer, it had not left its spiritual home. As it passed down and reached the sign of Leo, it commenced its apprenticeship for its approaching state on Earth.

The Solar Body, descending from the spiritual limits where the Zodiac and the Galaxy unite, loses its spherical shape, the shape of all Cosmic Principles, and lengthens into a cone, as a point is lengthened into a line.

And then, being the unitary Monad before it divides and becomes a Duad,--that is, Unity becomes division, disturbance, and conflict, resulting from the Principle of Polarity which inspires the struggle of the divided parts to re-unite.

Then the Soul begins to experience the disturbance that reigns in the Physical Realm, to which it joins itself, becoming, as it were
-42-

intoxicated by draughts of grosser matter, of inebriation, the Cup of Bakchos, the bottom half of the Zodiac called the Bitter Cup. It is for the Soul the Cup of Forgetfulness.

"The Souls (Solar Bodies) assemble in the fields of oblivion," said Plato, "to drink there of the River of Ameles, which causes the Soul of men to forget everything of its spiritual home." This fable is also found in Virgil.

Macrobius said, "If Souls took with them into the material bodies they occupy, all the knowledge which they had acquired of Divinity during their sojourn in the Spiritual Realm, men would not differ in opinions as the men's origin. But some forget more, and some less, of that which they had known.

We may smile at these material images and allegories, at the ideas of man struggling for utterance, the great speechless thoughts which they envelope,--but have we in modern times found any better way of presenting to ourselves the Soul's origin and its advent into the physical body?--Pike, 438.

The highest and purest portion of Matter, partaken of in Divine Existence, the poets termed Nectar, the beverage of the gods.

The lower, more disturbed and grosser portion, is what intoxicates the Soul. This the Masters symbolized as the River of Ameles, the dark stream of oblivion.

How can we explain the Solar Body's forgetfulness of its ante-cedents? or reconcile that utter absence of remembrance of its former state with its essential Immortality? It is largely due to the teaching and training men receive on earth.

Dragged down by the weight produced by this inebriating draught, the Soul descends along the Zodiac and the Milky Way to the lower spheres, and in its descent it not only takes, in each sphere, a new envelope of the material composing the bodies of the planets, but receives the different faculties which it shall express and exercise while it dwells in the material body, called man.

From the Sun it receives the senses and imagination, which pro-duce sensation, perception and thought.

From Saturn it acquires the power of reasoning and intelligence, or what is termed the logical and contemplative faculty.

From Jupiter it receives the power of action. Mars gives it valor, enterprise and impetuosity. Mercury gives it the faculty of expressing and enunciating what it thinks and feels; and Venus in-spires it with desires.

On entering the sphere of the Moon, it acquires the power of generation and growth.

The Moon, being the lowest and basest of the celestial bodies, is first and highest to terrestrial bodies. And the lunar body there assumed by the Soul, being, as it were, the sediment of ce-lestial matter, is also the primary substance of animal matter.

The celestial bodies, the Stars, the Planets, and the other divine elements, ever aspire to rise. The Soul, reaching the region inhabited by mortality, tends toward terrestrial bodies, and is fabled to die.

Macrobius said, "Let no one be surprised that we so frequently speak of the death of the Soul, which we call Immortal. But it is neither annulled nor destroyed by such death. It is merely imprisoned and enfeebled in the body for a time, and does not, thereby, forfeit its prerogative of Immortality. For afterwards, freed from the body by the process termed death, it is re-established in all its privileges and glories and returns to the luminous abode of its Immortality."

On its return journey to its Celestial Home, it restores to each sphere thru which it ascends, the passions, properties and physical faculties received from them in its descent.

The doctrine of the Pre-Existence of the Soul (Solar Man) as pure and celestial substance, is one of the very greatest of antiquity, a fuller discussion of which the reader will find in our Pre-Existence of Man.

Lactantius said that the Masters could not determine how it was possible that the Soul should exist after the demise of the physical body, if it had not existed before,--hence its nature was independent of the body.

Thus, the secret science and mysterious elements of initiation in the Ancient Mysteries were connected with the Soul, the Spheres, and the Constellations.

This connection must be studied by him who would understand the teachings of the Masters and learn how to interpret the ancient allegories any symbols, and explore the meaning of them, in which the Masters endeavored to delinate the thoughts that struggle within them for utterance, and could be but insufficiently and inadequately expressed by language, the words of which are images of those things that can be grasped by and are within the domain of the five physical senses of man.

The Universal Soul, motive power of the Macrocosm, receives its creative power chiefly thru the medium of the Sun, during its revolution along the signs of the Zodiac, with which signs unite the parenatellons that modify their influences, and concur in supplying the symbolic attributes of the Great Solar Luminary that regulates Nature and is the depositary of Cosmic Powers.

The action of the Universal Soul (Solar Body) is displayed in the movements of the Spheres, and, above all, in that of the Sun, in the successions of the risings and settings of the Stars, and in their periodic returns.

By these, according to the Masters, are explainable all the metamorphoses of the Soul, personified as Jupiter, as Bakchus, as Vishnu, or as Budda, and all the various attributes ascribed to it; and also the worship of those animals that appeared as Symbols in the Zodiac, and were consecrated in the ancient Temples, representatives on Earth of the Celestial Signs of the Zodiac, and supposed to receive by transmission from them the rays and emanations which in them flow from the Universal Solar Body.

In The Perfect Way, A. B. Kingsford wrote:

"The Soul is a Spiritual Sun, corresponding in all things with the Solar Orb. Wherefore, all they who, by virtue of their constituting for men a full manifestation of the power of the Soul, have been to them as a redeeming Sun--have been designated Sungods, and invested with careers corresponding to the apparent annual course of the Sun.

"Between the phenomena of this course and the actual history of the Soul there is an exact correspondence, requiring for its recognition but due knowledge of both.

"And it is because the Soul's history is one, and this is a history corresponding with the Sun's, that all those who have earned of their fellows the supreme title of Savior of men, have been invested with it, and represented as having exhibited the same phenomena in their own lives...and being the history of the Soul of the Man Regenerate, it corresponds to that of the Sun,--the vitalizing center of the physical system,--and has accordingly been described in terms derived from the Solar Phenomena as indicated in the zodiacal planisphere.

"Thus the Soul's history is written in the stars; and the heavens are her chroniclers....The Zodiac is the first and most stupendous of Bibles."

Crucified God Myth

The Crucified God Myth is another ancient symbol that represents a Cosmic Principle.

It symbolized the imprisonment of Cosmic Spirit in the Human Body, which occurs as the germ in the mother's womb expands into human being. Or as Cosmic Spirit envelopes itself in a Mantle of Matter called Man, formed by the materialization of Cosmic Rays, as explained by Prof. Lakhovsky in his Secret of Life.

Man's body, with arms extended and feet together, forms the Cross that was used by the Ancient Masters to teach the neophyte that we "hang on the Cross for evil purposes."

In other words, we use the body to satisfy our lusts for sensation, vanity, greed, hate, jealousy., hence we are "cursed" by our own conduct as physical beings. There is no other punishment.

The Masters taught that in producing Man, God sacrifices Himself by becoming a prisoner in the Jail of Matter that constitutes the body; and Man, in the production of children, also sacrifices his vitality and years of his life, as shown by modern science.

The Law of Compensation is universal and rules creation and production. Propagation involves compensatory sacrifice, which even God cannot escape. That is the ancient secret of God Sacrifice,-- another Cosmic Principle.

The ancient allegory of God Sacrifice for the sake of Man was literalized by the church in the 4th century, and used it for profit and power. Then it protects the fraud by controlling the Mind of its slaves. It bans books that teach the Truth which sets Man FREE (Jn. 8:32).

The esoteric phase of Ancient Philosophy involves Cosmic Principles and Cosmic Processes. That secret is concealed from the masses in the Zodiac and the Symbols of the Masters, and is revealed by a correct interpretation of Ancient Symbology.

Books on such subjects by orthodox Christian authors are purposely prepared to mislead and deceive, in order to hide the true meaning of Ancient Symbology and to conceal the Christian "Skeleton in the closet."

According to the Masters, incarceration of Cosmic Spirit in the Terrestrial Cross (human body) is the process that forms and fixes as an eternal entity, the Individual Consciousness of each person on the Astral Plane.

That is the purpose of living. That is the reason why man comes into being. That is the Cosmic Process by which Individuality comes out of Universality.

The Masters taught that, as a rule, Seven such incarnations are required to accomplish that definite state of Eternal, Individual Consciousness.

Seven is the number given in the Apocalypse, together with the Seven Sense Powers and the Seven Great Nerve Centers of the body, making Revelation the Book with Seven Seals, which no orthodox clergyman has ever been able to open (Rev. 5).

The Masters strove for such perfection of Mental Powers in the primary incarnation, that subsequent incarcerations of Cosmic Spirit in Matter were unnecessary.

Chapter 9

SECOND COMING OF CHRIST

The church fathers had to destroy ancient literature covering astrology and the zodiac to hide the nature and source of their "Lord and Savior."

"Behold the Lamb of God, which taketh away the sins of the world" (Jn. 1:29). Let us see where and how this Lamb of God fits into the ancient Picture.

In their study of Astrology, the Ancient Masters traced imaginary pictures all over the dome of heaven, to which the different stars were assigned. Chief among these, were the stars that lay along the path the Sun travels as he ascends toward the north in summer and descends to the south in winter,--lying within certain limits and extending equal distances on each side of the line of equal days and nights.

This belt, curving like a serpent, was termed the zodiac, and divided into 12 parts or signs.

At the vernal equinox in 4589 B.C., the Sun entered the zodiac sign and constellation of Taurus.

From Taurus, the Sun passed thru Gemini, Cancer, and reached Leo when he arrived at the terminus of his northward journey. Thence thru Leo, Virgo and Libra, he entered Scorpio at the autumnal equinox, and journeyed southward thru Scorpio, Sagittarius and Capricornus to Aquarius, the terminus of his journey south.

The path in which the Sun travelled thru these signs became the Ecliptic; and that which passes thru the two equinoxes, the Equator.

When the Sun began its trend southward, people north of the equator knew that shorter days, longer nights, much darkness, cloudy weather, barren fields, storms and cold were coming. This knowledge made them sad.

The Sun, the great regulator of mundane things and events, was the God of Light, of the Earth, of the Seasons, of the Harvest, of the People. Our God is a consuming fire (Ex. 24:17; Deut. 4:24; Ps. 50:3; Heb. 12:29, etc.) Without him, all were lost.

So the ancient Egyptians rejoiced and celebrated when the Sun, reaching its farthest point in the southward journey, seemed to stop and begin to ascend after the winter solstice, apparently struggling against the malign influences of Aquarius and Pisces, while amicably received by Aries, the Ram or Lamb, as "he, the Lamb of God, opened the equinox to deliver and save the world from the wintry reign of cold, darkness and barrenness."

This ancient celebration came down to us as Christ-mas, and, instead of the celebration being in honor of the birth of the Sun of God, it became the "birth of the only begotten son of God."

A little change in words makes a big change in meaning. It was that easy for despots to deceive the victims of darkness.

The earth entered the zodiac sign of Aries (Lamb) in 2,433 B.C., and the cycle extended to 276 B.C., when the cycle of Pisces began.

During the 2,160 years the earth was in the cycle of Aries, the Lamb was an object of great adoration when, in its turn, it appeared to open the equinox and thus "deliver and save the world" from the wintry reign of cold, darkness and barrenness.

And the people lamented when, after the autumnal equinox, the evil influence of the venomous Scorpio, the vindictive Archer (Sagittarius), and the ill-omened He-goat (Capricornus) appeared to drag the Sun down toward the winter solstice.

Arriving there, the Sun was fabled by the ancient Egyptians as being slain, and passed to the realm of darkness (Hades).

Remaining in darkness three days (Mat. 12:40; 27:63; Mk. 8:31), he rose (from the dead--Lu. 24:3) and began to ascend northward in

the heavens (Mk. 16:19), to redeem the earth and the people (savior
of the world) from the gloom, darkness and barrenness of Winter.
"Our Redeemer."

Thus the ancient Egyptians personified the Sun, and worshipped
him under the name of Osiris.

They transmuted the legend of his descent among the winter signs
of the zodiac into a fable of his death, his descent into the infernal
region, and his resurrection.

Now the time came when this fable evolved into a fact with
millions of people, and the fabulous part of the picture faded entirely from memory.

So Osiris (personification of the Sun) came to be regarded as
the God and Savior of Egypt, the masses forgetting that the mis-
fortunes and tragic death of Osiris, related in Egyptian scriptures,
were only allegory relating to the Sun.

In 1922 there was published the sixth edition of a work titled
"The Second Coming of Christ." The author was one Clarence Larkin,
and he began with the statement:

"There is no fact in history more clearly established than the
fact of the 'First Coming' of Christ. But as His 'First Coming' did
not fulfill all the prophecies associated with His 'Coming,' it is
evident that there must be another 'Coming' to completely fulfill
them."

Of course the many who have investigated the matter know that
there is not a scrap of reliable evidence on earth to show that such
a man ever lived as the gospel Jesus.

Christ's Second Coming is based on this statement which the
writers of the New Testament put into the mouth of their hero:

"In My Father's House are many mansions; if it were not so, I
would have told you. I go to prepare a place for you. And if I go
and prepare a place for you, I will come again, and receive you
unto myself; that where I am, there ye may be also" (Jn. 14:2,3).

This Second Coming is also mentioned in Acts in these words:
"Ye man of Galilee, why stand ye gazing up into heaven? This same
Jesus, which is taken up from you into heaven, shall so come in like
manner as ye have seen him go into heaven" (Acts. 1:11).

When Constantine founded the Roman State Church in the 4th century,
the fables of the nature gods of the Egyptians were literalized in
the New Testament, and Constantine "decreed as to how the N.T. Record
should be worded," wrote Livingston (Book of David, p.140).

So the church fathers adopted the fable of Osiris, worked it
over, and it became that part of the New Testament, the name of
Osiris being deleted and that of Jesus substituted, and the allegory
distorted to make the story of the Sun toil and travels appear as
those of a man.

-48-

But in preparing the N.T., the compilers were clever enough to make it contain dual messages, one for the esoteric and one for the exoteric, weaving their narratives around the symbolism of antiquity.

In this particular case they wove their story around the symbolism of the Zodiac, the ancient Wheel of Life.

The "many mansions" in my Father's House are the twelve houses (mansions) of the Zodiac.

The gospel Jesus here represents the head sign of the Zodiac,--Aries, Ram, an old Lamb,--the Lamb of God (Jn. 1:36).

When Jesus has twelve apostles, he represents the Sun of God, and the apostles represent the twelve "mansions" of the Zodiac. But when he is the head sign of the Zodiac, he has only eleven apostles. Ore had to be disposed of to make a place for him, and the church fathers very cleverly got rid of Judas, all of which is understood by the esoteric.

I Will Come Again

Now for Christ's Second coming: In its Great Circuit, the Earth passes thru the range of a Constellation, represented by a cycle of 2,160 years. In each Grand Cycle of 25,880 years the Earth passes thru all Twelve Mansions of the Zodiac.

This means that every 25,880 years this Christ (Aries) comes, and reigns each time for 2,160 years. Thus the biblical statement is true when properly understood.

The Earth entered Aries,in 2,432 B.C. From that time until 276 B.C. the Ram (Lamb) was the object of adoration by the ancients when, in its turn, it opened the equinox for 2,160 years,--

"To deliver the world from the wintry reign of cold, barrenness and darkness," as the ancients termed it in their annual celebration, which event the church adopted and Christ-matized.

During those centuries, the people living north of the equator called Aries "the Lamb of God which taketh away the sins of the world" (Jn. 1:29).

That is the correct interpretation of the statement, "I will come again." The Lamb comes every 25,880 years, and each time reigns 2,160 years.

Now for that "heaven" mentioned in Acts 1:11. That is just more spurious interpolation by the pious church fathers.

It is assumed the book of Acts was written by Paul. That is erroneous. The book was compiled by the church fathers from the writings of Damis, favorite disciple of Apollonius of Tyana, in which Damis described the work and travels of this greatest philosopher and teacher of the first century. This Damis (Demas) is mentioned in Phil. 24; Col. 4:14; 2d Tim. 4;10).

Let us assume that heaven, kingdom of heaven and kingdom of God are synonymous terms Of this kingdom the gospel Jesus said:
-49-

"The kingdom of God is like a grain of mustard, which, when sown in the earth, is less than all seeds, but grows and becomes greater than all herbs" (Mat. 13:31; Mk. 4:31).

The Luke says the kingdom of God is within us (17:21); and Paul (Pol, Polos, Apollo, Apollonius) said we are the temple of God, and the Spirit of God dwells in us (1 Cor. 3:16). Then at another time he said: "For the kingdom of God is not meat and drink; but right-eousness, and peace, and joy" (Rom. 14:17).

In other words, the kingdom of God and Heaven is a state of Mind, and not a place in space.

Biblical testimony directs us to look within the Temple of God for the Kingdom of God. But Catholics and Christians look for it up in the sky, like the men of Galilee who stood gazing "up into heaven."

Biblical evidence shows clearly that Acts 1:11 is a rank interpo-lation, inserted to mislead the "faithful" into forming an erroneous conception of the statement "I will come again."

The kingdom of heaven of the Ancient Masters was the Mind of man, the power of which is potentially omnipotent, omnipresent, and omniscient.

The Mind crosses the Time-Space barrier; it rises to the sky, to infinity, to eternity. Nothing can bar its passage. It pene-trates steel as readily as space.

Past and Future merge in the Mind and become the eternal Present. Eternity is here and now.

The old man looks back into the past and sees himself as a boy in the old swimming hole. The engineer gazes into the future and sees the skyscraper he plans to build, filled with goods and people.

Truth and Falsehood

It is almost impossible to read one paragraph in the Bible and find in it either truth or falsehood separately stated. Each false-hood is so inseparably connected with an undeniable truth, and the true and the false are so intricately and delicately interwoven, that is is absolutely impossible for the unprepared mind to separate the one from the other.

The Bible has gone out to the world and chained in darkness and ignorance a larger number of people than any other secular book has ever done, just exactly as was intended by those who prepared the Bible from ancient literautre.

These unfortunate victims must live in that darkness and error until they evolve to such mental ability that they can winnow the true from the false in this book and come to understand its falseness.

The Bible was compiled from ancient fables, and in order to interpret the fables correctly, one must know the substance of the teachings of the Ancient Masters.

It was for the purpose of hiding those teachings from the masses that the ancient literature was destroyed and the ancient libraries were burned.

Chapter 10

CHRISTIANITY

A full and correct account of the birth and reign of Christianity can never be written because its fraudulent nature caused the founding fathers to destroy the records.

1. The Christian Era may be roughly divided into five parts, the first extending from 325 AD to 500. That period witnessed the birth and establishment of the Holy Roman Church.

2. The next period, from 500 to the year 1000, was the Christian Nightmare. Not even the most ingenious Christian writer has been able to dissipate the darkness and mitigate the horrors of that real and only Christian Era,--when the Pope was the supreme ruler of Europe, and his bishops ruled the provinces of the Roman Empire, and grew rich on graft. Historians fix the 8th, 9th, and 10th centuries as the period of greatest darkness,--and the church was then the dominant power in that period.

3. The third period, from 1000 to 1500, is the Awakening from the Christian Nightmare. In the bloody struggle to hold its decreasing power, the church increased its work of slaughter and murder of "heretics."

This Age of Christian Savagery was followed by the Thirty Years War in Germany, which reduced the living standard of the German people to the necessity of eating their dogs and cats in order to survive.

Millions of heretics were executed, but not until the Spanish Inquisition in 1478 did church torture reach its climax.

Every instrument of torture that man could devise was used by the church upon those who questioned the church doctrines.

These outrageous tortures functioned until 1834. The executions usually took place on Sunday, amid great religious ceremonies, cal-culated to arouse the sentiment of the Christian mob against the victims.

By the middle of the 14th century, hardly a hundred years after the first Turks had pitched their tents in Mesopotamia, the Mo-hammedan civilization was so much superior to that of Christendom, that thousands of Greek and Roman Christians fled to it and embraced Islam, to escape from the terror and horror of the "perfect religion" called Christianity.

4. The fourth period, from 1500 to 1800, is the real discovery of the Christian fraud.

In that period Martin Luther started the revolt which led to the birth of Protestantism, which is just a branch of the main trunk of Catholicism, somewhat modified from the original.

In its bloody battles to hold its fading power, the church murdered millions of "heretics." In Spain alone, between 1600 and 1670,
the church inquisition burnt alive 31,912 "heretics."

Queen Isabella, writing to the bishop of Segovia of her work to
promote Christianity, said, "I have caused great calamities. I have
depopulated towns and provinces and kingdoms (by having people
slaughtered) for the love of Christ" (Hist. of Inqui. p.124).

Hordes of Huns, Goths and Vandals were imported from the north
by the church to replace the murdered population. They were permitted to enter and take possession of the property of the slain
upon taking an oath to believe in the gospel Jesus and support and
defend Roman Catholicism.

That is the real story of the Fall of Rome. The false historic
account prepared by the church is the one that Gibbon wove into his
works. Whether he knew the actual truth probably no one knows.

By 1816 outraged public sentiment rose so high against the
murderous work of the church, that a papal bull was issued, "to put
an end to torture and death at the stake for opinion's sake" (Wall,
p.341).

As a result of Luther's courageous work in the 16th century,
Europe began slowly to arouse from the death-like trance resulting
from church authority.

For more than 1200 years the church had reigned supreme over
Europe. The Pope was the dictator not only of man's religious life
but also of his political and intellectual activities.

Men were denied the right to think outside of the narrow limit
of Christianism. If they did, they were tortured and burnt "at the
iron stake for opinion's sake."

A book on Canon Law, approved by Pope Leo XIII, says, "The death
sentence is a necessary and efficacious means for the (Catholic)
Church to attain its ends."

With the establishment of the church in the 4th century, all
schools were closed, libraries demolished, research work banned, and
science was branded as "magic."

The church promptly dug the grave of Ancient Wisdom, and banished
the ancient philosophic forms of culture, poetry and science, while
the Initiation Drama of the Ancient Mysteries was anathema.

In the 4th century all search for truth and knowledge came to
an end. The church would tolerate no scientific study and research.
The church led men away from the Masters of the ancient world, and
from the ethical rituals of the Mystery Schools, which for ages
had disported their educational and philosophical dramas in the
great temples of Egypt, Asia Minor, Greece and Rome.

The church scorned the Wisdom of the Ancient Masters, and ground
their science and philosophy into dust with loud cries of "heresy."
It scoffed at secular learning, and civilization plunged blindly

forward under its control and leadership into the greatest abyss of darkness and ignorance that man has ever known.

In the so-called Middle Ages appear a series of lurid pictures in which the Lights of Ancient Wisdom flicker out, one by one; all the way from the days of the First Council of Nicea in 325 AD, thru the Crusades, the "Holy Inquisition," the persecution and slaughter of "heretics," to the days of Queen Elizabeth of England (1533-1603).

During these dark days of church dominance, no intellectual and scientific activities were permitted. In the 11th, 12th, 13th, and 14th centuries the people of Europe sank to the very lowest ebb of thought. The social life of the masses was wretched in the extreme. The majority of the people lived in hovels of squalor and filth. The laboring classes were regarded as serfs of the church. To them were unknown the glory of ancient Greece and the grandeur of ancient Rome; while the great land of Egypt was branded as the "Land of Darkness."

During these dark ages, when filth was sacred to the church, epidemics, plagues and physical distress in Europe took millions of lives. By the 13th and 14th centuries, people were perishing so fast that the plague was called Black Death,--a condition that Christian historians falsely allege originated in Asia and spread over Europe.

The plague was almost continually present in London until late in the 17th century.

Out of this state of misery and distress was born another fraud, termed Medical Art, which attempts to justify its existence by pointing back to the condition of the people in those dark centuries.

In time this fraud became a "profession," and the great Dr. R.T. Trall wrote that it was a sad day for humanity when that occurred.

Science Disappears

After the wanton destruction by the church of Ancient Science and its valuable records, the Sun of Science sank to rise no more for a thousand years.

Then came Copernicus, Galileo, Bruno, Kepler, Descartes, Newton, Buffon, Goethe, Lamarch, Darwin, Spencer, Huxley, Haechel and Fiske.

Galileo swept the sky with his telescope and said, "The World Moves." Darwin examined the animals of earth and ocean and showed that all living creatures are related, and live and move and have their being by reason of a common Creative Power.

These astounding discoveries shocked the Christian world, and were met by the church with a storm of obloquy, abuse, ridicule, and scorn. No one should believe them; they were preposterous. If you did believe them, it was at the risk of your life.

With the persecution and slaughter of those who attempted to develop a science, it was not until the 17th century that science began to bud, at the time when church power had begun to decline. The vanguard of this budding science was imprisoned and burnt to stifle the revival of learning. -53-

After Servetus, Bruno and Galileo, there came the archeologists, who began digging in the ruins of ancient cities and temples, most of which ruins were the work of the church.

The discoveries of the archeologists amazed the world. They found that 2000 years before the earliest writings of the Old Testament, there had been inscribed on Babylonian bricks the same stories of Creation related in Genesis, of the Flood and Noah and the Ark, with depictions of a man, a woman, a snake and a tree.

Doom of Christianity

5. We now reach the fifth period, which began about 1881, when the Earth entered the Air Sign of the Zodiac.

This period has already witnessed the destruction of a large part of the papal dominion, and a shocking decline in church attendance.

One writer declared that in the USA less than fifty million persons belong to church; while Dean Inge, famous spokesman of the Church of England, said: "Doctrinal Christianity is doomed."

Another writer said: "The reign of Christianity as a system of doctrines is over."

The press of July 9, 1948, quoted the Bishop of Norwich, Dr. P.M. Herbert, as stating:

"The great number of churches standing dusty and unused all over England is scandalous."

He made no estimate of the total number of empty churches, but cited examples. In his diocese, he said, there were three idle parish churches within a quarter of a mile of each other.

Prof. Barry E. Barnes shows in his work, "The Twilight of Christianity," that it has entered the declining stage.

Ernest H. Cherrington, who reviewed and criticized Barnes' book, admitted that the reasoning and logic of Barnes are sufficient to demolish Christianity, and would lead to atheism.

How can there be a sensible, logical, reasonable argument against a "perfect religion" established by God?

Evolution

The birth of the theory of Evolution in the 19th century was the result of the Mind of man emerging from the fog of the Dark Ages and grasping anything to replace the ridiculous anthropomorphic God of Christianity.

With Ancient Wisdom lost, without any knowledge of Cosmic Science, the budding of modern science regarded the theory of Evolution as the answer to the mystery of Creation, and caused millions of thinking people to turn from "doctrinal Christianity."

-54-

Now the evolutionists find themselves embarrassed by the great
discovery in the field of atoms, where visible substance is found to
be nothing more than condensed Electricity, and the Spiritual World
of the Ancient Masters beginning to appear as a reality.

Chapter 11

THE LONG DARK NIGHT

To remain ignorant is to remain a slave (Wayland).

Enlightened people are difficult to enslave. Despots want slaves;
so despots hate enlightenment.

Why is ancient history so fragmentary? Why have we so little
knowledge of ancient races and their civilization? Why have we a
most none of ancient Egypt?

Why did Archbishop Chrysostomus boast in the middle of the 5th
century AD, "That every trace of the ancient philosophy and literature
has vanished from the face of the earth?"

Why did the church fear the printing press when its invention
made it possible to supply the world with books?

The then Bishop of London in 1474, in a convocation to his clergy,
said, "If we do not destroy this dangerous invention, it will one
day destroy us" (Bible Myths, p.438). He voiced a prophecy that is
coming to pass.

If you are of that class which obeys the church order forbidding
the reading of certain books, this work is not for you; for the Facts
it contains would strike you dumb.

This work is intended for that small class of sincere folks
earnestly seeking Light and Truth, and not for the gullible masses
that are looking for evidence to support what they are taught. Blind
belief in popular teaching cannot face cold facts.

If this were the 17th century, and this author lived in Europe,
he would be burnt at the stake as an enemy of God.

It has taken one thousand six hundred long years to do it, but
diligent archeologists have finally dug from ancient ruins that
damaging evidence which exposes the most colossal fraud in all the
annals of history.

It was in the year 325 AD when the button was pushed that plunged
all Europe into the blackest night the world has ever known.

The man who pushed that button had just become the despotic
ruler of the greatest empire since the sinking of Lemuria in the
Pacific 15,000 years before.

Constantine the Great, mighty ruler of mighty Rome, hands red
with human blood, had just gained the throne of the mighty Caesars,
and was determined to be in history, greater than the Great Julius,
who made the charming Cleopatr Queen of Egypt.

Teachers of Truth and Virtue may be great men in their work, but what they teach is so undesirable in a World of Fraud, that these men are never great in the eyes of the world, nor in the pages of history.

Being only human, intoxicated with his success in slaying his rival, Maxenthius, and craving greater power, Constantine decided to rule the religious life of his subjects as well as their politcal life, never realizing of course that he was starting a movement which would ruin the very empire of which he was the proud ruler.

With his plans before him, in 325 AD Constantine called that now famous convention of the leading bishops of his realm, which became known in history as the First Council of Nicea. The evil that grew out of its work will continue to blacken the pages of human life for centuries yet to come.

The purpose of the convention was to "invent" a New Religion that would give the despot greater power over the people. For good reasons a report of the proceedings of the council was never made public. But fragmentary references to the proceedings, contained in private letters of many who attended, show in substance what was done and how.

The New Religion was invented in a very easy manner. It was accomplished by simply literalizing the leading fables of the ancient religion, and personifying its principal symbols.

The New Religion became known as Roman Catholicism, and its spread over the Roman provinces was vigorously pushed by those put in charge of the campaign.

When it became known at Rome what had been done, it made Constantine so unpopular that he found it expedient to move his headquarters to his new city of Constantinopolis on the Bosphorus; and that is why and how the latter city became the Capitol of the Roman Empire under Constantine.

This fact is not correctly recorded in our histories and encyclopedias, for they give the world only what the church ordera and permits.

Prof. Max Muller wrote: "Beware of all versions of history that come from Christian hands."

It was not easy to force on the people of the countries under Roman control, the New Religion with its utterly unknown and strangely "crucified god," who was wrapped in swaddling clothes and laid in a manger when born (Lu. 2:7, 16).

Helena, mother of Constantine, being deeply interested in the matter, was unable to find in all Jewry anyone who had ever heard of this "crucified god."

Some think that may be the main reason why Constantine had her assassinated. The New Religion had to be protected at all cost.

T. W. Doane writes: "Not so much as one single passage purporting to be written as history within the first century of the

Christian era, can be produced to show the existence at or before that time of such a person as Jesus of Nazareth, called the Christ, or any such set of men as could be accounted his disciples or followers" (Bible Myths, p.564).

The Rev. Dr. Giles says, "Great is our disappointment at finding nothing in the works of Philo (Jewish writer contemporary with the gospel Jesus, about the Christians, their doctrines, or their sacred books.

About the books we need not expect any notice; but about the Christians and their doctrines, his silence is more remarkable, inasmuch as he was about sixty years old at the time of the crucifixion, and living mostly in Alexandria, so closely connected with Judea, and the Jews could hardly have failed to know something of the events (recorded in the gospels) that had taken place in Jerusalem" (Hebrew & Christian Records, vol. 2, p.61). They never took place.

When the strange story of the gospel Jesus was first introduced among the Greeks and Romans, they were inclined to mock at the "Lord and Savior" of the manger. That mocking ceased as they discovered how dangerous it was when the Emperor promulgated the Faith in official decrees, which the police and soldiers enforced

Little did these Greeks and Romans dream that they and their children, for fifteen hundred years, were fated to see rivers reddened with their blood because of the gospel Jesus whom they had mocked, while their proud Empire would crumble into dust and darkness as the Roman Hierarchy rose in power, and, with Bible in one hand and bloody sword in the other, gradually clamped its galling yoke upon the countries controlled by Rome.

Little did Paul (Apollonius) and his group know that "the gospel which was preached of me is not after man" (Gal. 1:11,12), would be revised and revamped to make a man of a mystic symbol, the Spirit (Sun, Spark of Life) in all men (Col. 3:11), and make the Spiritual Resurrection to which he referred as a mystery (1 Cor. 15:42, 51), the literal resurrection of a human corpse.

What a shock it would have been to Paul had he known that the kingdom of God which he declared could not be inherited by "flesh and blood" (1 Cor. 15:50), and which the Luke said was within man (Lu. 17:21), would later receive into its folds the "flesh and blood" of the gospel Jesus, who is made to say,

"Behold my hands and my feet, that it is I myself; handle me, and see; for a spirit hath not flesh and bones, as ye see me have" (Lu. 24:39).

The Ancient Religion, which had prevailed in all parts of the world for a hundred thousand years, had to be suppressed; ancient history and philosophy had to be destroyed; ancient temples had to be razed; the Masters of the Ancient Religion had to be converted or assassinated.

Regardless of all this, the work was done and done well. Many of the Masters fled to mountainous regions, and there continued their great work in secret.

-57-

The task of burning literature, suppressing learning, and murdering dissenters continued and advanced, until by the middle of the 5th century the "dark ages" were rapidly settling over Europe.

Bolingbroke says, "The scene of Catholicism has always been one of dissention, of hatred, of persecution and blood." Look at Europe even now and see how true that is.

Erasmus wrote, "The church was born in blood, grew in blood, succeeded in blood, and will end in blood."

Tredwell pointed out that Catholicism forced its way forward by the suppression of philosophy, by mass murder, and by the point of the sword.

That is how the "Church Militant" was born and how it developed into a world power, reaching the heights of its success in the darkest days of its reign.

In relating a brief account of that horrible event, James R.L. Morrell writes: "It is a strange and amazing history I have to tell, but it is true--every word of the charges I made. It is an account of the deliberate and malicious corruption of the most ancient and honorable religion in the world. It involves the interpolation and destruction of a vast literature and, finally, the ruin of one of the greatest civilizations ever known in order to cover up the crime. So successful was this work carried out, that few people of today ever suspect the colossal humbug that was played upon the world."-- Spiritism and Beginnings of Christianity, p.1

Then came the journey of Columbus in 1492, showing that the earth is round, not flat as was taught by the church. That knowledge electrified the world, and flew so fast that it could not be suppressed. It created the very condition that Romanism had foreseen when it did all in its power to prevent Columbus from making the trip.

This was the actual beginning of the reformation, the renaissance. It was bitterly fought by Romanism, but the battle was lost, and Enlightenment began to scatter the darkness.

Prior to the invention of printing, all books were written by hand, making copies expensive and hard to get. It was easy for the books of the Bible then to be kept from the people. Furthermore, reading the Bible in those days was prohibited by law, and translations had to be made secretly for fear of the consequences. So the Bible passed into comparative obscurity. The rank and file knew nothing of its contents.

With the reformation and the invention of printing, it became harder to keep the Bible from the people. The Reformers at once set about translating it. Luther in Germany; Tyndale and Coverdale in England; Olivetan in France succeeded during the 16th century in placing versions of the Bible within the reach of the common people.

After several intermediate versions, the present English "Authorized Version" was first printed in 1611, a little more than three centuries ago.

We have presented in this work some facts concerning the ancient religion, called Paganism, that are known to few people.

As these facts unfolded, we are amazed to learn how deeply the old Masters had dug into the mysteries of life thousands of years ago, and to see how skilfully they concealed their discoveries and knowledge in symbolism and allegorism.

It was the personification of the symbols and the literalization of the allegories that gave the world the New Religion. It took the best brains of Europe hundreds of years to do it, but the work was so dexterously done that even now it is practically impossible to persuade most people to believe that they are the Victims of the most nefarious fraud on earth.

Struggle for Light

When you have read our ten works presenting the Lost Knowledge of the Ancient Masters, you have entered a new school of thought, in which you will discover a new world, which was the antediluvian college of Natural Science, in which the Masters revealed to man the secrets of his own origin, and the nature of his being.

While this philosophy may be new to you, it is as old as the race, and was, or Paul (Pol) declared, "Preached to every creature under heaven."

It was carried to Egypt before that land had a name, by the Masters who survived the Flood of Noah, and preserved in symbol and allegory for the races of the future.

As you proceeded thru the work you discovered why the Masters concealed their wisdom from the world at large by mysterious symbols, parables, fables, fiction, and other means.

You also discovered why you will remain in darkness as long as you believe only in the visible world, and see in the Bible only the written word.

The written word was prepared to mislead the profane who were not prepared for the facts of Life.

To him who is guided by appearances, the Sun seems to rise in the east, sail thru the sky, and set in the west, never realizing that each rising is a setting, and each setting is a rising.

In like manner, to those guided by appearances, man seems to come into being when he is born and to come to an end when he dies. And such is the teaching of modern science.

Modern science is in darkness because its leaders live by sight and think accordingly.

The members of the church are in darkness because they believe in a savior and the vicarious atonement, and are offended by reason, facts, truth.

Constantine began the work in the 4th century that produced the

Dark Ages when he crushed the Ancient Science and founded the Roman State Church.

The Dark Ages reached their zenith in the 15th century when the church had reached its greatest power. That power began to wane and the darkness to fade in the 16th century, when courageous men preferred burning at the stake to remaining longer in darkness.

But the battle for Light has only begun. The church is fighting fiercely to recover its power, and physical science is fighting hard to sustain its theory of Evolution.

At this hour intelligent men in the USA are rotting in prison, while others are being silenced and liquidated, for the "crime" of opposing the teachings of the church and science.

The Life of Apollonius; The Hidden Life of Jesus; The Council of Nicea; Falsification; The Legend and the Truth Interwoven - Why?; The Mystic Sleep; The Second Coming; The True Understanding of the Biblical Statement. Many reject this book at the first reading - later they come back to buy scores to give to their friends. It is a book which will change your entire life. The author says: "TRUTH is such a rare quality - a stranger so seldom met in this civilization of fraud, that it is never received freely, but must always fight its way into the world." Get this book now - read it - and you'll probably become another follower of Hilton Hotema.

www.ingramcontent.com/pod-product-compliance
Lightning Source LLC
Chambersburg PA
CBHW060636280326
41933CB00012B/2060